TOKKIE SMITH
AND THE COLOUR OF RUGBY

Creating the Hong Kong Sevens

© 2018-2025 John D'Eathe
www.tokkiesmith.com

John D'Eathe asserts the moral right to be identified as the author of this work.

All rights reserved. This book or any portion thereof may not be reproduced or used in any manner whatsoever without the express written permission of the publisher except for the use of brief quotations in a book review

Creator: D'Eathe, John, Vancouver, author.

Production editor: Kevin McDonald

Title: Tokkie Smith and the Colour of Rugby. Creating the Hong Kong Sevens

Second Edition ISBN 978-0-9919930-8-6

Subjects: Rugby union, Hong Kong, England, South Africa, apartheid, Hong Kong Sevens

Most pictures have been provided with thanks by Tokkie's friends and fellow players. Others from that time period are taken, with permission, from the Hong Kong Football Club's ....*along the Sports Road*, and from Hong Kong Rugby Football Union's *The Hong Kong Sevens* published in 1985. It is believed all picture copyrights have been sought and received but the publisher welcomes further information on this subject.

Cartoon reproduced by permission of Andy Neilson.

FRONT COVER PHOTOGRAPH: Courtesy of Hong Kong Rugby Union

TOKKIE SMITH
AND THE COLOUR OF RUGBY

Creating the Hong Kong Sevens

By John D'Eathe

who introduced new rugger pal Tokkie to his colleague Vernon
Roberts at the Gloucester Hotel on December 4, 1959.
That is really where it all began.

Dedicated to Dr Will Jones, late of Port Macquarie in
Australia, a dashing scrum half and pal of student days,
then family man, dedicated surgeon, life-long friend
and always a hilarious raconteur.

ABOUT THE AUTHOR

AUTHOR John D'Eathe is a product of the golden amateur period of rugby. He has seen the game transform from elitist and non-inclusive into the brilliant, open Sunshine Rugby of today.

He met Tokkie Smith in 1959 in exotic Hong Kong and joined him for a decade in the waning days of the British Empire and of Colonial rugby. He played regularly for the Club, a few times for Hong Kong and has a Blarney Stone Sevens tournament mug. He lost out to concussion and took on the HK Rugby honorary secretary role during the opening up of the game, leading later to the establishment of the Asian Rugby Football Union. He mixed with the amateur Old Toffs still running RFU from England.

He moved to Vancouver but continued rugby friendships that have helped him research this book. He looks back objectively and sees the impact his friend Tokkie Smith had upon world rugby.

Many influenced change but Tokkie was special with his life totally committed to the Game, progressively including different peoples and nations. Perversely his liberal attitude caused his downfall and personal tragedy.

In the crowning achievement of his life, his insistence upon the Sevens game being played and upon multi-racial inclusion, produced the Hong Kong Sevens, which he organised and managed in its early years. It was this critical and exciting turning point in the international rugby paradigm for which he deserves the credit.

Author John D'Eathe asserted for many years that Tokkie Smith was an un-sung hero of today's all welcoming game. He is pleased that Tokkie has now taken his rightful place in rugby history.

TABLE OF CONTENTS

Part 1	Makee Learnee	 9
	Chapter 1	The Gloucester Bar........... 11
	Chapter 2	Frillies 16
	Chapter 3	A Son of England 20
	Chapter 4	Getting it in London 24
	Chapter 5	The Fading Empire........... 31
Part 2	Hong Kong	 39
	Chapter 6	An End to Isolation 41
	Chapter 7	Opening up the Game 45
	Chapter 8	I Zigga Zumba 50
	Chapter 9	Tokkie Gets Sophisticated...... 53
	Chapter 10	Goodbye White Rugby 60
	Chapter 11	The All Blacks 63
	Chapter 12	The Need for Sponsors 68
Part 3	Uniting Asia	 71
	Chapter 13	Joining the Establishment 73
	Chapter 14	Last of the Amateur Toffs 78
	Chapter 15	Family Affairs 82
	Chapter 16	The Roberts Era 91
	Chapter 17	Finally, England 94
	Chapter 18	Tokkie Takes Over 99
Part 4	Founding the Sevens	 105
	Chapter 19	Big Money 106
	Chapter 20	Decision................... 111
	Chapter 21	Founding the Sevens.......... 116
	Chapter 22	Old Friends 121
Part 5	Apartheid	 131
	Chapter 23	Prestigious Years 132
	Chapter 24	A Return to Africa 137

"It was the most colourful day of sport that I have ever seen. One that puts Hong Kong on the international sporting map."

– Tokkie Smith
after the first
Hong Kong Sevens
in 1976.

Chapter 25	A Good Try	142
Chapter 26	Secret Plans.	147
Chapter 27	The Brilliant Islanders.	153
Chapter 28	Finding the Dragons.	156
Chapter 29	A Secret Arrival.	161
Chapter 30	'A Worthwhile Exercise'.	167
Part 6	**Judgement**	175
Chapter 31	The Reckoning.	176
Chapter 32	Alone	186
Chapter 33	The Morning After.	190
Chapter 34	A Rolling, Bouncing Ball	196
Chapter 35	Final Whistle	203
Chapter 36	Redemption	206
Acknowledgments		212

The colonial rugby elite sat in stunned silence. He had been accused but not heard. Never before had they been required to make such an emotional and personal decision. Slowly, one by one, they raised their hands and his life was over.

Part 1

Makee Learnee

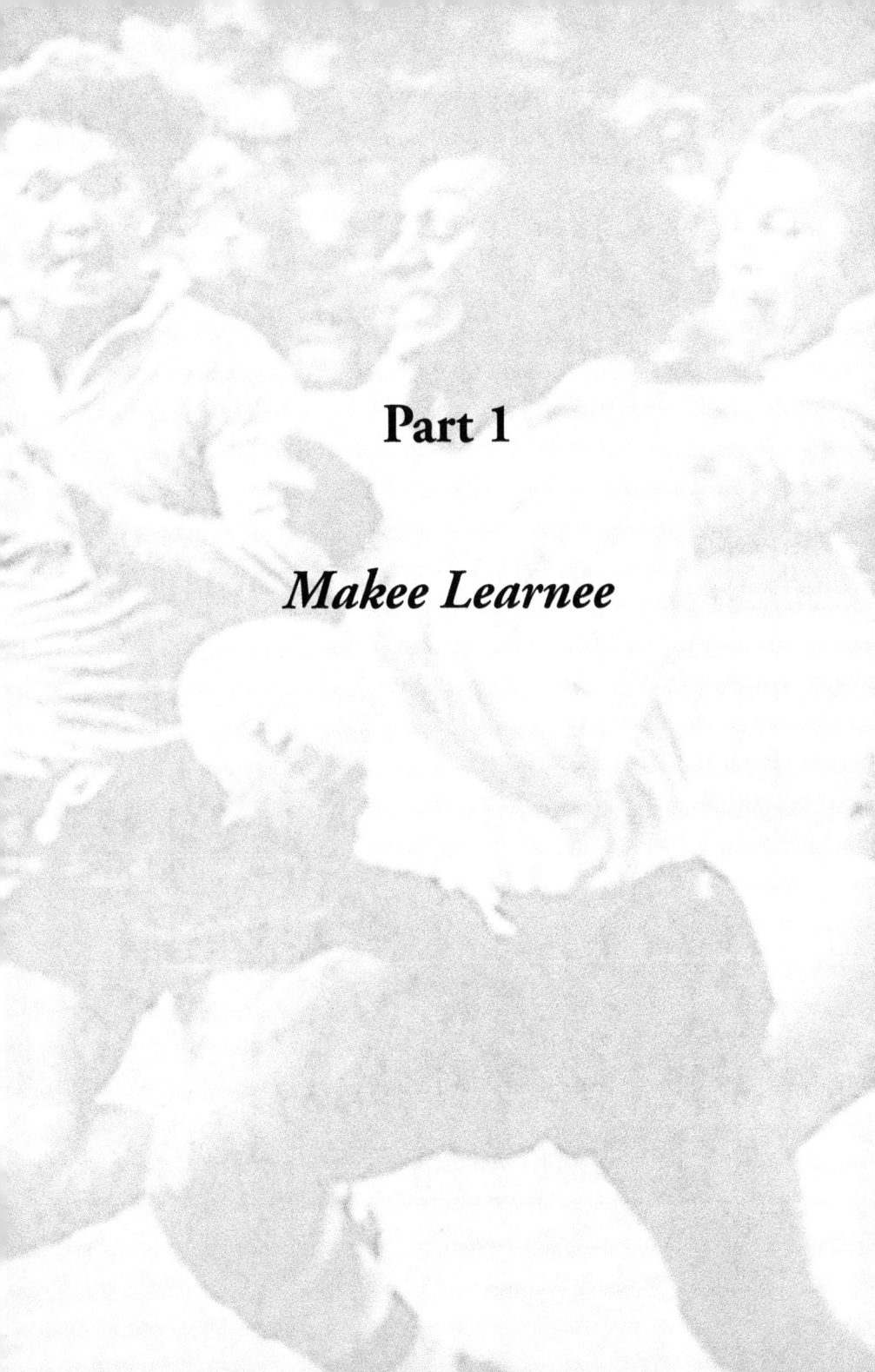

The Gloucester Hotel ... where it all began.

1

The Gloucester Bar

THE Hong Kong rugby establishment had retaken the top floor bar of the Gloucester Hotel from the Japanese army at the end of the Second World War.

During the occupation, the hotel in central Hong Kong had been the abode of the feared and deadly Japanese officers. The bar boys, afraid of evil spirits, still claimed to hear screams after dark from the interrogation dungeons below.

None of this apparently bothered hotel manager Vernon Roberts, who had fought the Japanese through Burma and up Malaya with the fierce Ghurkhas and stayed on in the Crown Colony.

It was Vernon and his influential friends 'Tokkie' Smith was seeking.

He first strolled around Hong Kong towards the end of 1959. It was not like anything he had experienced. This was culture shock.

He was accustomed to seeing mostly black people but suddenly he was totally surrounded by Chinese faces. The Cantonese language was loud and raucous. They all seemed to shout. The air was hot and humid, and had a distinctive Asian aroma.

His clothes clung to his back. Traffic belched smoke everywhere, the green trams squeaked and clanged, and the ferries disgorged

Feared Japanese officer rides at the rear.

Vernon Roberts introduced Tokkie to the rugby elite.

thousands of passengers in a continuous stream.

Everywhere there was noise and excitement.

The harbour-facing city itself was a mellow pile of old three- or four-storey buildings, some actually quite beautiful, mainly of pre-war Asian colonial design but with nodes of modern higher buildings shining through.

The air of excitement came from the tens of thousands of people flowing in from Mainland China and desperate for work. He saw this as an opportunity.

Tokkie's first stop had been the Football Club Bar where his new friends insisted he must be introduced to the girls at their favourite Wanchai bars. He found the saucy little bar girls to be a real novelty, but he needed to concentrate on finding work.

The fellows suggested if he really intended to start a company he should go to the Gloucester and meet the older rugger crowd with the money.

They could be found in Vernon Roberts' bar.

The Gloucester Arcade was in the business area at the centre of all the action. The cacophony of traffic, trams and teeming, shouting people still assaulted his ears.

Then the uniformed lift boy clicked the metal door shut and he ascended in silence to the air-conditioned peace of the smart, top floor hotel lounge.

> **He saw no Chinese players at the Football Club**

He strolled out of the lift into the realm of the Hong Kong establishment; a lair of the rugby elite that from that moment would dictate his very life.

Totally assured, he went to the bar, ordered a San Mig and asked for Mr Roberts. Then he beamed and in a strong South African accent announced, "My name is Tokkie".

In his mid-20s, he was tall and burly, full faced and with an easy grin below a trimmed, blond moustache. Very relaxed, he had an air of self-confidence about him.

He listened seriously to the guys at the bar with his eyes narrowed; his forehead and eyes crinkled in interested concentration.

Using rugby as an introduction, he told them his first beer at the Football Club Bar had been bought by a Scottish fellow called Denny, then by an Aussie called Digby and he tried to remember the others – Les, John, Tommy, Hector, David, Duncan.

Now at the Gloucester Bar he was soon chatting about the game

Gerry Forsgate goes to Japan and helps resume peace through rugby

and was immediately accepted on a first-name basis. He tried tactfully to get the subject around to business, but when he said he was in ladies clothing it raised such a laugh that he returned quickly to rugger.

Tokkie's game in South Africa and England had been among the elitist white society. However, he said he had played with Maoris in New Zealand and heard tales of the nearby Pacific Islanders' exotic style.

The Gloucester Bar drinkers admitted the local game was confined to expatriates, but countered that it was widely played by many races throughout Asia.

He listened with fascination to Gerry Forsgate's account of the Colony side he had captained on a tour to Japan soon after the war.

Why did they want to play rugby with such a vicious enemy accused of so many atrocities in Hong Kong? Well, they explained, they had to start somewhere and this was one of the first efforts to start rebuilding relations.

What better reconciliation than a game of rugby and a few beers; leading to improved trade, of course! It had all started happily enough for Tokkie. Vernon and more new bar companions with names to remember listened to his happy tales about rugby life in South Africa. He waved his glass and insisted earnestly that the Springboks were clearly the best team in the world.

"So, why do you only select white players?" they demanded. "I haven't seen any Chinese fellows at the Football Club," he responded defiantly.

That had raised the whole subject of apartheid and racism generally. Here, he said, he was finding even the meaning of racism to be totally different.

At home there was clearly colour sensitivity involved, but it was mainly a matter of different cultures and economic control. He thought it inevitable that sooner or later they would sort it out. Anyway, they all played rugby.

In Hong Kong people of many backgrounds seemed to live happily and equally together, and were only interested in business and making money. So long as the government and the courts ran things fairly and they were safe, he had not met anyone concerned about racial differences or even interested in politics.

The Chinese knew themselves to be superior and again it was only a matter of time. Look at what had just happened in Singapore where the local chap, Lee Kuan Yew, had become Prime Minister and was running full internal self-government. For the moment, Tokkie could not join some of their clubs here and they could not join some of his. No, the situation in South Africa was totally different.

"Sorry we asked," they laughed and brushed him off as a *makee learnee*.

2

Frillies

IN 1959, the British Empire was still very much in existence, at least in many colonial minds. Hong Kong was a relatively insignificant crown colony, coping with the negative effects of the changing political arrangements on the Mainland.

China had cut itself off from the world, with the Great Leap Forward, whatever that was, hidden from view but reportedly underway. That communist fellow Mao Tse Tung had been in charge there for more than a decade and was still firmly in control, but things apparently were not going so well.

As a result people had been illegally flowing out of China and the population of Hong Kong had grown quickly to an unprecedented three million people. Many were living in mountainside shanty town slums or hastily built, nasty concrete resettlement buildings.

Far away from the hillside squalor, Tokkie awoke in comfort, to the clanging of the trams in the street below, and to the sharp click clack of the workers' wooden clogs before plastic soles brought comparative morning peace to the city.

The territory was far more isolated in every sense than it became and the economy was in a slump. Things moved slowly then. In his normal business it would take him a month to exchange letters or

This was culture shock ... rickshaws and all.

documents with a contact in Europe or North America.

Tokkie saw an opportunity in the cheap but skilled labour becoming available and moving out of China.

He hoped to import selected items of quality goods as a wholesale agent – ladies clothing for his friends back at Pringle and more manly gentlemen's items for Dunhill – then start manufacturing and trading generally.

The world had not yet developed an international tourist industry. Hong Kong was a mysterious destination and certainly not a place you would visit casually.

China would not even seem to exist except for the flow of refugees. It was a massive, brooding presence just up the Pearl River and over the horizon. Exotic Macao was an easy boat trip across the delta, and great for a quickie weekend. Canton was a forbidden city.

Tokkie had arrived economy by air, with help from Stockland and Ferguson a British firm with whom he intended to associate. Before he could even get started he must rent a central district showroom, which was totally out of his reach. That little problem was easily solved by his new rugby pals at the bar who were in the real estate business.

He was so happy to get premises that he signed the lease with barely a glance, laughing that he was a concepts man and not into details, a characteristic the establishment would later rue.

With business taken care of, Tokkie was looking for a flat so he could bring his wife Dilys to Hong Kong. He was still alone and Christmas looked bleak until original bar companion Denny Johnston invited him home for the dinner with his wife Lena and their young family. Denny was to prove to be his genuine and constant friend when most others had turned against him.

By the new year, Tokkie was proudly established in his small Central showroom, with smart new showcases displaying the frillies, blouses, scarves and whatever other female unmentionables he was offering for wholesale distribution.

China had cut itself off from the world.

He was already accepted both in business and in the rugby crowd. He could drift confidently into the Gloucester Bar and the downtown Cricket Club. Of course, he was a regular at the bar in the Football Club in Happy Valley.

He had no problem getting into the swing of a few drinks at lunchtime which was the general way of life.

His new rugger mates could have guessed from his assured talk that young Tokkie Smith soon would be the club and colony skipper, but not that he was destined to become a rugby legend!

The old Football Club men's bar (above) and an aerial shot of the rugby stadium.

3

A Son of England

WHEN he was born in 1934 in East London, South Africa, he was given an impressive name: Arthur Donnison Cooley-Smith. His English-speaking parents were both from Smith families who had been on the Cape for at least three generations.

Arthur's earliest memories were growing up in his liberal, pro-English household. His father, demonstratively an Anglophile, was in the 'shipping business'. The country was bitterly divided with the National Party gaining control and pursuing increasingly racist policies.

Great social change was underway across the world. After suffering centuries of domination, people everywhere were taking control of their own destinies.

The young Tokkie was brought up as a staunch Brit, secure in the fact that the Empire was still intact. In those years before the Second World War, the Brits were still running or controlling upwards of an amazing 60 countries and territories, although now more tactfully called a Commonwealth.

He had learned in school that the Empire had moved to Commonwealth in 1931 when Canada, Australia, New Zealand and South Africa had become self-governing Dominions. His Dad said that was when all the trouble had started and he would sneak off to quiet meetings of the Sons of England.

The Sons of England Patriotic and Benevolent Society was founded in Cape Province in 1881. They hid behind a facade of supporting "English traditions and good ideals and raising funds for benevolent purposes", but were really a semi-secretive political organisation.

More to the point and publicly they maintained "equal rights and opportunities for English-speaking South Africans" and promoted "amenity, peace and unity among citizens of all races in Africa". This brought them trouble from the National Party in the badly divided country.

> **People everywhere were taking control of their own destinies. This notion seem to have bypassed racist South Africa.**

He learned to be proud of his father's political stand but not of the way he treated his mother and the family. To a large degree the Sons were a cover for Dad's carousing and fun with the ladies.

Arthur was just an impressionable 14-year-old when the National Party gained control of the country in 1948 and imposed apartheid. To add to his personal problems his mother left his clearly alcoholic father when he overdid it and got too obviously involved with another woman.

She took Arthur and his little sisters to live in Durban and ended up working to support the family. His mother's family name before she married also had been Smith. She dropped the name distinction and chopped off Dad's hyphen on account of his misbehaviour.

Thus, in Durban, just in his teens, he became Arthur D. C. Smith.

He later joked that as a little boy he had been chubby and always stuck in the front row. By the time they moved to Durban and he reached the Under-15s he was growing taller and becoming faster and he went to lock, which he considered a promotion.

As a sign of his future capacity he was soon appointed captain. Although youngsters, the all-white players were trained to play a tough game aimed at always winning.

He was banged about a lot and even his mother was worried about his trips to hospital and his several concussions. He was told to wear a scrum cap but stubbornly he never did.

The vast population around him was not white and he naturally met lots of other kids and people who were outside his white social set. The problem was that because of segregation he was never given the opportunity to play rugby with them or really get to know them personally.

As apartheid developed his mother became more distraught and kept saying they would have to leave. His teen life became one of tension and uncertainty.

The government brought in the Population Registration process by which everyone was classified by race. Then apartheid removed civil and political rights; restricted access to land and economic opportunities; stopped inter-racial marriage; and reserved good jobs for white people. Every day they seemed to think up a new racist restriction, enforced by increasingly and necessary police military repression.

Tokkie was very aware that apartheid would change his life because his mother was despairing for South Africa and on school holidays always threatening seriously to leave.

Sports enthusiasts of all races had engaged in cricket and rugby which had been taken around the world by the colonialists since the 1880s and widely seen as the controlling white man's sport. It became a sign of prestige throughout the Empire to play these games and especially to be invited to join the actual expatriates at their games.

South Africa had rugby organised in racially separated administrations from the beginning although there was a certain amount of interplay. Strict separation was imposed by the adoption of apartheid in 1948 when black players became second-class citizens barred from the best facilities, trainers and competitions frequented by whites.

The story went right over Tokkie's young head when, the following year, Danie Craven was appointed the Springbok coach, totally and vocally agreeing with these segregationist policies. The scene was set for South African rugby for decades to come.

At the time Doc Craven was reported to say that black players would be selected as Springboks over his dead body, which fairly clearly stated his position. He was to have a dramatic effect upon Arthur's later life.

Tokkie was soon relieved to be sent off to board at the prestigious, very English, South Africa College, in Cape Town, finally being supported by his father. He was thus away at college and somewhat isolated in his white community from the upheaval brought about by the criminal imposition of apartheid from 1948. And they lived rugger!

With the innocence of youth, however, in this sad atmosphere he completed school in Cape Town going on to play for Hamiltons RFC in Cape Town and Berea Rovers in Durban. Then, considering himself grown up, at 19 he made the gutsy decision to move to London on his own.

He was very proud of his cadet military commission with the Queen's Own Cape Town Highlanders and amused his friends and family by proudly parading about in his Scottish regalia. They suspected he went to London really to see the coronation parades and the young Queen Elizabeth.

4

Getting it in London

WHEN he arrived in London Tokkie had developed into a tall, handsome fellow who was very gregarious and made friends easily. He immediately discovered the pubs and strangely ended up playing a few games at London Irish with drinking buddies.

He found everyone in London still buoyed up by their victory in the world war less than a decade earlier. He was appalled at the extent of the devastation and damage from the bombing which was evident everywhere but saw it all being enthusiastically rebuilt.

Arriving from quite parochial South Africa he revelled in the feeling of confidence and power at the centre of the Empire. He perceived Great Britain still as the most powerful nation on earth, even with loss of India after the war, controlling some 50 other territories and directing commerce around the entire world.

Then came Queen Elizabeth's coronation on June 2, 1953. Tokkie waited for hours in the deep, happy crowds lining the streets of London for the ceremony and colourful parade.

The very latest tannoy technology provided a public sound system broadcasting the proceedings. A rolling cheer swept through the streets at the timed announcement that Edmund Hillary and Sherpa Tenzing Norgay had conquered Everest.

Then the long parade went into full swing demonstrating Britain's heritage and power despite gathering rain clouds. He applauded with everyone as the popular Queen Salote of tiny Tonga clattered by in her ceremonial horse-drawn carriage. She endeared herself to the crowd by refusing cover, waving and beaming through the entire parade in the pouring rain.

Tokkie would have been amazed to know that decades later a critical decision on a rugger field in a free Tonga would totally disrupt his life.

The crowd all hushed to hear the Westminster Abbey coronation ceremony over the loudspeakers and joined in the wild crescendo of cheering as the newly crowned young Queen rode by in her sensibly covered carriage. That day Tokkie truly felt a Son of England.

Confidence and power at the centre of the empire

He then set out to discover London, but got far more than he expected. One evening friends introduced him to a beautiful, sexy, young woman visiting from Australia. The sights of London got lost in his whirlwind romance with the experienced, five-years-older Dilys. Later he very sensibly married her.

His mother and two little sisters emigrated and also arrived in London. He decided on a business life and signed on to study marketing and textiles at Selfridges. Getting established, he moved on to play at the more prestigious Blackheath Club.

He found the rugger clubs a bit snobbish and class conscious. It helped that he had been to a boarding school but he was amused that his South African accent left them puzzled and perplexed as to his class.

London was a highly cosmopolitan city and he found himself rubbing shoulders with people from all over the world in the city's myriad bars. For the first time in his life he realised racial prejudices disappeared with friendship, preferably nurtured over a few beers.

He used his textile education and took a job offered back in South Africa but immediately found the social restrictions too stifling after London. He had always thought about a military career and one day he noticed an advertisement offered the opportunity to join the New Zealand Army.

This was in a different world, but it apparently had an army and it certainly was a rugger country, so why not?

Taking advantage of his school cadet commission and proud of his kilt and full regalia, he decided on a military career, with a commission of course.

He hopped on a plane and went all the way to Auckland for an interview. Once there he found they had changed government and stopped recruiting, so he never actually joined up. He did stay, missing most of the season but enjoying the odd game including with the tough Maori players.

New Zealand denied a white policy but did maintain a quota immigration system in common with other western countries which could euphemistically be called selective because there were very few Asian or Pacific Island faces to be seen.

That served immigration but within the country he knew there was only limited discrimination with respect to the Maori New Zealanders who had the protection of treaties. It was totally different from home because the large majority here were white and clearly in control.

Tokkie's first love Dilys.

Still, the Maori friends he met at the rugger club were just regular guys and lived normal integrated lives. He scrounged a few games. It was not in season, but he could boast playing with the tough Maoris.

Far from lording it over others with his commission he found himself labouring and doing any jobs to get by. Within a few months he tired of construction work and moved on to look around Australia.

He had been concerned they might be heading the same way as South Africa when he had heard about the White Australia Policy, but he found that this was progressively being dismantled and that the country was accepting immigration from many races around the world.

It was obvious the Australians were all pretty much white as was their rugby. They were clearly losing out to the Kiwis who boasted Maoris in their teams!

He did not stay around long to find out too much because he heard that his father had finally overdone the partying and had died. So once again with a quick decision he jumped on a plane and headed back to South Africa.

> **The Kiwis had the advantage of Maoris**

He stayed on and worked in textiles again for a couple of years in South Africa, having fun playing rugby for Berea Rovers in Durban, the Harlequins in Pretoria and on trips to Rhodesia.

But apartheid and the oppressive scene wore him down. When the National Party outlawed *God Save the Queen* it was too much and he knew it was time to go.

■ ■ ■

But go where? Back in London, trying to decide, a trade contact at Stockland and Ferguson asked whether he would be interested in representing them in the expanding Hong Kong market? "Where exactly is that?" he enquired

Thus, it was indeed an adventure, late in 1959, when he ended up in the colony, aged 25, now married to Dilys, determined to start a business, and looking for Vernon.

CREATING THE HONG KONG SEVENS

Along the way Arthur had picked up the name Tokkie. It is a common Afrikaans word for a beetle. As a young child in the East Cape he had played a game called tok-tokkie – knocking on front doors and running away.

For whatever reason, that nickname stuck. By the time he got to Hong Kong he had totally given up on Arthur and always introduced himself as Tokkie.

The name was very distinctively Cape which obviously pleased him. Accompanied by his earnest expression, serious eye-to-eye contact and firm handshake, "My name is Tok-Kie", pronounced in his very South African accent with equal emphasis on the "Kie", was something you remembered.

He started training seriously at the Football Club early in 1960 but was dismayed at the easygoing approach to the sport. He complained to Aussie captain Digby Bennet that rugby in Hong Kong was just a local fun game played between white gentlemen.

He had found the ground was usually rock hard and was embarrassed by the suppurating sores that stuck his thighs to his lightweight trousers all down his legs during the hot weather.

He laughed at reports from England that his prized Springboks were in trouble on tour for winning their games through rough-housing and thuggery.

His happy wife Dilys arrived in the new year and quickly

Dilys and Tokkie ... joining the social and business set.

Dilys, Jenny Bennet and Tokkie with new club captain Digby Bennet.

became part of the rugby crowd. She was outspoken and knowledgeable about the game. She was tall, complementing her husband, good looking and energetic.

Dilys fitted in very well with the expatriates. She was beautifully mannered, calm and although you could hear she was Australian she spoke with a moderated English accent. This all changed once she was a regular in the football stadium with her girlfriends, having fun and all bellowing advice

They soon became aware that "anyone who was anyone" was in the rugger crowd, but that they must pay due deference to their politically well-placed senior colleagues. This was the social and business set they must join.

Almost everyone they knew lived in an apartment and having a house was a sign of great success, especially on The Peak. Finally they had an invitation to a mansion, occupied by a new South African buddy who ran a large transportation corporation.

After dinner, the ladies retired to their drawing room for tea and perhaps a giggly liqueur. They were expected to discuss family and domestic affairs, tiresome servants and, of course, the latest gossip. They had many Chinese female friends but actively protected their menfolk from any liaisons with these attractive women. Other socially aspiring young women might have their aspirations dashed by a casual, "You do realise she is Chi Chi?" or "Of course, her mother was a Shanghai White Russian".

The men, formally attired, headed off to the library for discussion of serious topics of colonial importance over brandy, port and cigars.

But first, a long-established colonial ritual. In older mansions plumbing was limited and the men trooped out into the warm dark garden and lined up at the edge of the lawn to pee into the bushes.

"I've arrived!" thought Tokkie, happily sprinkling their prize hibiscus.

5

The Fading Empire

THE cry of "boy" was still often heard from the imperialists in bars and restaurants, particularly to call for another drink, after several.

The summons was used in a somewhat friendly but demanding manner and the "boy" could well be an old and faithful retainer. Dominant status needed to be demonstrated in the waning Empire and it was good at least to feel you were still superior.

Behind their backs they were called Gweilos with dismissive sighs and befitting sniggers.

Since his childhood, Britain had 'lost' a dozen of its territories to self-rule although they did not count because they were mainly cricketers. Britain still controlled more than 50 territories.

Still, the move to freedom was well underway and Tokkie recognised the Empire's time was clearly up. More important, what would this mean for the game?

Rugby was traditionally the sport of the white imperialists, and at least in Hong Kong he found things proceeding as normal with some 20 teams dominated by the Club, the Army, RAF, Navy and the Police, who played the pentangular tournament, plus upwards of a dozen friendly and regimental teams.

There were selected teams to take on any visitors and play local

All good fun. After matches the focus turned to the Men's Bar.

But the party soon moved to other settings

tournaments, such as the Taipans game. Just all good fun and heaven forbid anyone gets hurt. Then off for a shower and a good evening drinking and singing at the bar.

All very colonial and expatriate, of course!

The Men's Bar was the choral centre of the colonial rugger crowd and while only really a chorus man, Tokkie joined in enthusiastically but not musically. He knew a few verses of *The Wild West Show*, *Balls to Mr Bangelstein* and *Lily 'Awkins*, but mainly followed the prompting of choirmaster Chris Rowe.

He would thump the bar and call for a traditional recitation from the *Book of Kings* in which Daniel famously refuses the King's call for a general act of defaecation and is cast into a den of lions. When Daniel outwits the King, Tokkie would join in the shouted punch line, "And the laugh was on the King".

Then the call might be for one of Tokkie's infamous 'tramp' stories, all based upon a similar faecal topic, with the whole bar belting out the appropriate punchline such as "Oh, I though you meant today", accompanied by boos and cheers.

The docking of a British or New Zealand warship did bring new songs and stories, and indeed added the colourful Maori to the bar and football pitch. Also they brought fresh competition and much harder games.

Particularly feared by the gentlemen players were the New Zealand frigates *Otago* and *Rotoiti*. When they moored, first down the gang plank was their rugger squad on a training run. This was serious stuff and Hong Kong's only regular window on international rugby. A 'passive' war was raging between Malaya and Indonesia increasing British forces in that area and bringing an Aussie and Kiwi military presence to South Asia.

This meant some very tough rugger teams.

The permanent players in Hong Kong were destined as they aged to

Future Union colleagues Newbigging, Smith. Johnston and D'Eathe join the Club team.

become part of the establishment. They became long-term employees in government, police and business, all staying around for a career. They then retired back home in their 50s providing a steady rugby management turnover.

Tokkie found the 'stop-over' military, RAF and naval fellows at HMS *Tamar* to be incredible drinking types. Many of the military and naval officers tended to speak with exaggerated English accents that took him a while to understand, but their mess parties could be wild! His friends multiplied: Spike, Charlie, Steve, Kit, Terry.

As a frustrated would-be soldier Tokkie encouraged friendships with these military types and was regularly invited to their mess dinners. All male and in their dress kit, they started out very formally, leaping to rigid attention at the entrance of the Colonel. The evening often degenerated into wild but always correct irreverence as the drinks flowed.

At a Dining Out for a popular colonel who was leaving the colony, long after the Loyal Toast, of course, Tokkie assisted in hoisting the inverted burly commanding officer so he could march across the ceiling and leave his blackened bare footprints for posterity.

Tokkie was proud to be part of developing the esprit de corps of the British colonial army.

More mundane, but no less character building, were such mess games as British Bulldog and High Cockalorum which involved teams racing around the dining room without touching the ground, by jumping on each other's backs or the furniture. Or Moving Billiards where the white ball had to remain in motion with team players taking alternative moving shots and with obstructive body blocking allowed. He was finally participating in military traditions that had built the Empire.

Not yet on the selectors' list, Tokkie watched helplessly in December as a laidback Hong Kong team was thrashed by visiting RAF airman from Singapore. Times were changing and the hot rumour in the bar was that the visitors had arrived in their own aeroplane for the game!

Tokkie always claimed that local rugby finally started moving out of the gentlemen's era in March 1960 when the Colony team played the visiting Commonwealth Brigade from Malaya. This was the combined Australian and New Zealand military side which boasted an international star backline, plus three All Blacks.

> The Sevens was already a local tradition played at the Football Club stadium.

The band and drums of the Cheshire Regiment set the military scene. Governor Sir Robert Black, a Scottish rugby enthusiast, had the teams formally introduced.

Sir Robert was a modest gentleman, often seen in his raincoat watching local games from the back of the stand. Now he sat grandly at the front, where he belonged.

It was a brutal contest which "degenerated into a near brawl", according to the local newspaper. Two colony players were carried off, one to hospital. Of course Commonwealth Brigade won, but barely.

CREATING THE HONG KONG SEVENS

This all fitted in with the way rugby was changing internationally, with more determination to win. The Springboks had demonstrated this on their tour of the United Kingdom that year as had the New Zealanders and Australians on previous tours of Britain.

Tokkie sat fuming in frustration in the stand as Hong Kong was manhandled. However, that did not affect the after-game festivities. That was where the bar friendships developed with Aussies and Kiwis. These were beginning to shape his life and would later change world rugby.

At the end of his first season he discovered the Blarney Stone Sevens. The Sevens was a local tradition, played at the Football Club's stadium over several days with some 14 teams taking part. The first Sevens had been played at the Football Club in 1932, in aid of charity and continued, except for the break during the Japanese occupation.

Club members had ordered the distinctive Blarney Stone Shield from England in 1934, prophetically the year Tokkie was born.

In a few months, he had emerged as a strong club player and was selected in the Sevens A team. He adored the openness and pure fun of Sevens and pushed the club into special tactical training for the event.

The club did not win the shield in his first year, but as a consolation he bought himself a totally impractical 1953 Open 2.5 litre Riley car. A real clunker and petrol guzzler but totally fitting his larger-than-life personality and moustache.

He polished that car and drove it around Hong Kong's narrow roads with a broad smile for years; to Dilys's chagrin.

Soon after, in April he was up on the table with others telling jokes at the usual raucous closing steak and kidney dinner at the club. A beaming Tokkie posed for the first time in the Football Club team photograph, together with all his new friends, several of whom were to join the rugby elite and feature in the later drama of his life.

He was not much of a movie man, but Dilys dragged him to see the *The World of Suzie Wong* movie when it was released that year. It immediately turned Hong Kong into a 'go to' tourist destination.

While it dramatised the existing packed hillside squalor, it showed high life in the colony, portraying slinky cheongsam-clad women, streets of colourful bars in Wanchai, swinging nightclubs, crystal-clear waterfront and beach scenes, and endless cocktail parties.

They got it just about right!

CREATING THE HONG KONG SEVENS

Part 2

Hong Kong

CREATING THE HONG KONG SEVENS

6

An End to Isolation

ALREADY asserting his authority in the clubhouse, Tokkie became club vice-captain in his second season. In that amateur sport there were no coaches, so the captains ordered the drills. The gloves were off; gentlemen players no more!

Trevor Bedford arrived and quickly became a great pal and rival, toughening up the team and later being an influential rugby leader.

Meanwhile, Pringle sweaters and 'spangles' were selling well. Spangles, because Tokkie had come up with a brilliant idea that delighted Pringle back in Scotland: to have cashmere sweaters deco-

Tokkie up and Jack Johnston responds for the police.

Service provided by houseboy Peter and Amah.

rated with sequins in Hong Kong. His friends still found it incongruous to see his big hands gently folding beautiful, soft ladies wear!

He had begun travelling around Asia, particularly north to Taiwan and Japan trying to set up his trading and import/export business, particularly working rugger contacts whom he found very compatible.

He aspired to a flat on The Peak where the successful lived and with the help of teammates in the real estate business he found a good deal. Very soon he was able to move Dilys up into the mist.

Back home in South Africa there were abundant working people and he had grown up accustomed to home help. In Hong Kong apartments had amah quarters and if you could afford it, room for a houseboy.

He found them more skilled, much more expensive but good humoured. For example there was the houseboy who retrieved and next day re-served the awful inedible Mooncake he had proudly made to celebrate the Chinese Autumn Festival, which they had thrown out the window so as not to embarrass him.

There was no humour in the deformed feet of his wife, the amah. They had been bound to be small as a young child in the interest of beauty, leaving her hobbling painfully around the dining table.

The British Navy was still a great force in the world and the China Seas. In mid-November the Navy had enough ships nearby to put together a Far East Fleet team good enough to beat the Colony.

Tokkie trained hard and was determined to get into the Colony

Vice-captain Tokkie moves up.

selection, but the very tall Army pair Spike and Charlie had a lock on the second row. Those were the days before the fancy practice of grasping firm thighs and lifting to get height. The second row actu-ally had to jump for the ball. Tokkie joked that he could do with a couple more inches; with a twinkle in his eye!

A few months later he was flush-faced and excited the morning he finally heard he had made it into the Hong Kong side. It was enormously important to him. Rugby was his life.

A mixed race team from Saigon.

He did lose in that first Colony game against Singapore Military Services. He admitted very privately he had only made it in because Spike and Charlie were off fighting a war somewhere. But he got selected!

There were in fact real wars around. The French were still holding

The military second row wedding of the year.

on in Vietnam, but sent the Saigon Rugby Club on tour. This was Tokkie's first experience with mixed-race teams from Asia which were to heavily influence his life. Saigon surprised him by stretching the club and barely losing to the President's representative side.

Now living like a gentleman, Tokkie had access to a garden and they could have a dog. He was soppy over that puppy and named him Chaka after the Zulu king. He was in private a very gentle person, easily moved emotionally and openly pleasant and courteous.

However, his self-assurance could over-assert itself particularly as he saw everything in black and white. Then he could be intractable, plain frustrating and capable of flying into a heated rage over apparently unimportant matters.

Although he claimed to have worked hard at it, Tokkie and Dilys were not destined to have any children. The Smiths quickly settled in, developed a wide circle of friends and were very popular.

He was upset when 'his' Colony team narrowly lost to the strong visiting New Zealand Regiment from Malaya and he was determined to toughen up the training. It was clear the Kiwis played a far more aggressive game.

He pointed out that if he had joined the New Zealand Army he could well have been on the winning side.

7

Opening up the Game

ONCE again Tokkie happily welcomed the 1961 Blarney Stones, his favourite time of the year! He had no idea this would be the year the sun would shine through on local rugby.

As a sign of good things to come, his own first seven, picked for speed and obviously expatriates, were knocked out in the first round by an absolutely novice mixed-race Recreio Club team. Mixed race?

He was initially annoyed but back in the bar, seeing the flushed faces of the excited Recreio team, he recognised a wonderful change was taking place.

The main factor that had held back local people, as compared to expatriates, from playing rugby was a bias in colonial prejudice and exclusive club attitudes. Or the dismissive, "They are not interested".

The Recreio Club had a long and distinguished history in the Portuguese settlement of Macao, established 300 years before the British drug traders seized Hong Kong as a base.

Over time the Portuguese had intermarried with local folk producing a proud group of mixed-heritage generational residents. In those race-conscious days they were somewhat defensive.

By the time Tokkie came on the scene much of that old prejudice had gone, but the separate clubs still existed.

Thus everyone at the Football Club had applauded when Club

CREATING THE HONG KONG SEVENS

Recreio makes history.

Tokkie meets an all-Chinese team.

Recreio announced the formation of a rugby section and their intention to contest the Blarney Stones. It was their ability and success that shocked!

Several local Hong Kong Bank employees who were Recreio members had been invited into the Waifoong 'Bank' team earlier in the season and the idea caught on. Traditionally the team had been made up of expatriate 'bank boys' many housed in the Bank Mess.

Tokkie's side did not expect to be beaten by them in the first game! The Recreio team ran hard and threw the ball about with abandon catching Tokkie's over-confident team flat-footed.

But that is what happened and here was Tokkie and the Club first team later singing along in the Men's Bar doing what Tokkie believed in: making friendships through drinking beer together.

Recreio's triumph was short lived and they were knocked out in the next round by the Club Dragons who had the advantage of having seen them play.

Dragons had several Colony-selected players and used their experience and weight to win. Aggressive forward play, backs lined up defensively, work the line, and use the offside law tactically for advantage.

> **For the first time he personally came up against an all-Chinese team.**

Tokkie hated defensive tactics. "Open it up," he shouted from the stand, giving a boost to his new friends Recreio. The Dragons were booed all three days of contest and excoriated in the press but they stuck to that game plan and won the shield. Recreio for their part reported a very satisfactory start and their intention to field a full team the next season.

The emergence of colourful Recreio was a new experience for local rugby and for Tokkie personally, but at the end of that season, he had another. For the first time he personally came up against an

Finally he's captain ... Tokkie's getting serious.

all-Chinese team. This was a brief visit by the Taiwan RU team whose tough, fast, smaller players almost upset the club. He was surprised and learned a big lesson that day not to underestimate a smaller team. Also he was told there were now 30 teams in Taiwan.

In autumn 1961, Tokkie finally headed the Club team and was elected captain. Club Recreio fielded a mixed-race side and after training all summer, took on the Club Dragons. This time Club was ready, played a tight and tough forward game with a defensive backline to win convincingly.

The writer 'Prop' ran the headline "Recreio XV beaten but not disgraced in first appearance", and reported they were going on to a three-days-a-week training regime. They had started a new era and had become colourful regulars at the club bar after games.

With an ignoble start as skipper, Tokkie led Union and Club teams off on a disastrous tour of South-East Asia. The Colony lost to Saigon and only beat the tiny Penang club. In tougher competition the Club could not beat any of Cercle Sportif Saigonnais, Bangkok or the University.

He was learning the hard way that Asians could play great rugby but he was sure making a wide variety of new friends. His excuse for the losses was that they were too well entertained. Indignant, he protested that there were different people at the lavish, boozy parties than the next day on the field; poor dears!

Tokkie found that throughout Asia, clubs were looking for more international visits and competition. With more long distance tours the HKRFU was becoming increasingly influential.

In June 1962 rugged Police Commissioner George Wright-Nooth, became chairman. George was a very tough cop, rumoured to have executed Central District snipers sympathetic to the Japanese cause, personally and on the spot, as the island came under attack.

Somewhat less dramatically, he tried to persuade the annual meeting to introduce memberships fees at HK$100 for life. He was himself shot down; too expensive.

As jugs of beer were circulated the members noisily advocated that the union take more initiative internationally. The secretary was instructed to contact all Asian clubs to set up a more formal regional association.

As even more beer circulated, it was also agreed to invite team visits from outside Asia, especially from Australia and New Zealand, to capitalise on the many personal friends made through the military games.

In the following months all those contacts were made and HKRFU was setting itself up to be the focal point of rugby in the region, and for the formation of an Asian Rugby Union.

8

I Zigga Zumba

TOKKIE was relieved after all those tour losses to be again elected Club skipper for the 1962-63 season. He was a commanding player always up with the game shouting instructions, a tough fighter for the ball and the Club's consistent and majestic touch kicker.

That summer, before the season, he took Dilys back on leave to South Africa, switching hemispheres to avoid the humid Hong Kong weather.

No one anywhere thought of Hong Kong as a rugby destination, so he missed the incredible news of a touring side coming from Europe. Long union negotiations had paid off and the Paris University Club had agreed to add Hong Kong to their Japan tour.

I Zigga Zumba ... en Francais!

Early, in humid August the training started. Then with little warning the massive Typhoon Wanda hit, causing widespread devastation and killing some 50 people. Training and trials carried on through the heavy rain, but captain Tokkie was still in South Africa.

He arrived back mid-September just in time for the final trials and to meet Pierre Beteille, Paris University's manager, on a pre-game visit.

Kim exchanges pennants.

Pierre, who had become Tokkie's friend and contact in France, was a French cap. He said he would field up to eight French internationals plus a visiting many-capped Scottish international. No wonder they were a little reluctant to play the Colony!

Tokkie made it into the team but as a blow to his self-esteem the Colony had appointed Club player Kim Robertson as captain in his absence.

Kim was an absolutely charming bank employee and very tough scrum half. This was a wonderful moment for Kim but one about to be overwhelmed by tragedy.

Paris University were a wild bunch at the end of a strenuous tour. At every public event several of them got up on the table and performed a 'sexy', full French strip accompanied by the *I Zigga Zumba* team song. Just coming back from the Transvaal, and very aware of the enormous turmoil the hated apartheid was causing, Tokkie loudly applauded their choice of the Zulu warrior chant.

At the Chinese restaurant welcoming dinner, the agitated pro-

A tough Colony side.

prietor became very alarmed at the sight of several very big, hairy and naked men dancing on the table. He shouted he was calling the police. "I am the police," boomed George Wright-Nooth, the Police Commissioner and Union chairman, singing along enthusiastically.

Governor Black provided more dignity, greeting the visitors formally at the opening game ceremonies. The very tough game against the Paris University ended in a draw. Kim at scrum half took a pounding from the quick and big French loose forwards, which later became very significant.

George Wright-Nooth.

There were speeches and songs in slurred English and French at the robust dinner in the Football Club dining room. The entire PUC team were up on the tables for their *I Zigga Zumba* finale.

If only the world knew Hong Kong was a fun place for rugby fans.

Further, would the Union ever make so much money from a game? The committee was delighted to bank a remarkable HK$5500 proceeds.

Unbelievable!

9

Tokkie Gets Sophisticated

THE HKRFU committee held their normal informal meeting at the Club bar emboldened by the PUC visit from Europe. Now they also had lots of money in the bank. Why not convince the England RFU touring side to stop in Hong Kong on their coming tour Down Under in May 1963?

There was not even a glimmer of interest back from London. Someone did acknowledge the letter; that was a start.

Locally, the Far East Fleet put a team together for a Colony game in January 1963. The mighty little HMNZS *Taranaki* warship arrived fielding several tough Maori and gave Tokkie's Club side a vicious, hard game. They were so aggressive they demanded to play the Colony.

Tokkie was becoming aware of the toll the increasingly serious, 'all-out-to-win' games were having on his gentlemen players. There were mounting injuries and concussions and it was seriously debated around the bar whether the risk of toughening up the Club game was worth it? Some employers were also getting concerned.

He realised he had to change his attitude towards referees when he raised dangerous play in the usual after-game friendly banter in the bar about the laws of the game with Doc Walter Allright, the doyen of the whistle men. Walter had founded the Refs Society a few years before

CREATING THE HONG KONG SEVENS

*Above: Centre of attention Bill Riach who was soon to die in an accident.
Right: Tokkie argues with referee Harley.
Below: Frisby meets Robertson.*

and they were formally recognised with a seat on the Union board.

He insisted on high quality performance, study of the laws, taking tests to qualify, the instruction of players and, unbelievably, actual running and physical training.

Further, they had opened the game to a Chinese referee, deep rugby thinker Bill Leong. He was cerebral, firm and popular, and absolutely added colour to the staid white group of refs.

While bridging no dispute on the field, the other regular senior refs, Alan, Henry, Brian, John and Tokkie's particular friend Tommy Harley, often had heated bar battles after the games over some disputed decision or other.

Tokkie had pretty much considered refs part of his playing problem. Now he was beginning to appreciate how essential high-quality refereeing was to attracting great teams to play in the colony.

To this point in his rugby career most of his interest in the game had been on the field but now as a team leader he was getting stuck on committees and becoming involved in policy and administration.

The 1963 new year brought an important international breakthrough with RFU for Hong Kong and started giving Tokkie his first personal connection with the top brass.

H.R. 'Frizzles' Frisby, the President of Surrey RFU and a very influential member of the RFU board, was on a business trip, visiting ref Tommy Harley at Jardines to discuss insurance. Just out of interest he decided to check out Hong Kong rugby.

Frizzles wanted to meet players, so there was a large bar gathering. Of course he attended some games, there were reasonably serious committee meetings and the case was made strongly for more stopovers by international teams.

At the formal dinner for Frizzles at the Hong Kong Club the Union was making every effort to impress! Tokkie was decked out in black tie for the special occasion and commented on the dinner for years to come. However his memories did not centre on Frizzles.

The Colony skipper Kim Robertson give the formal speech of welcome to a beaming Frizzles. Kim was wearing dark glasses and his face was heavily bruised. This became very significant to everyone very soon after.

Frizzles became a friend to visit and an important Tokkie contact at Twickenham. Already then an older guy, and one of the disappearing old toffs, his career had been in City of London insurance.

As an apprentice he ran out to fold down the steps on the horse-drawn carriages and to assist the clients alight. He had seen rugby develop from a minor sport.

A fascinating bullet-headed man with many stories to tell, over many beers, he and Tokkie were rugby fanatics who hit it off immediately.

A favourite story from his Hong Kong visit came from a newspaper report then about an unfortunate local Hong Kong businessman who had misbehaved, and while he was asleep his wife chopped off his penis.

Back in the UK after a Surrey RU game, Frizzles entertained his team and their debutante girlfriends to cocktails at his home. He told

Cozying up to the RFU

his new Hong Kong story and a wide eyed sweet young thing exclaimed in horror, "What, right through the bone!"

Tokkie retold this ad nauseam as his story turn in the Club bar, to the generally shouted punch line, "Right through the bone". In fact it became his forwards' rallying cry!

The Union committee had to decide how to capitalise on the Frisby visit. They had not given up on an England stopover on their pending tour Down Under. With Frizzles' help a reply was actually extracted from the RFU President himself, who only offered Micky Steele-Bodger, celebrity and rugby writer, as a consolation prize. Vivian Jenkins later turned up, but it was a start.

Old gent Frizzles.

Tokkie had concerns other than rugby but his business had prospered and he now had a smart showroom.

His trading contacts had expanded meaning more visits to Japan which complemented his rugger interests.

More Japanese and Taiwanese teams

He had already palled up with English-educated Shiggy Konno who was beginning to administer rugby in Japan having assisted the Oxford University tour in 1952.

They discussed how recently they had been at war. Shiggy had been trained as a kamikaze pilot and told the tale of having his deadly flight scheduled for one month after the war actually ended! A month later and Japan would have been short a prop forward!

The subject of shamateurism was just arising, because although rugby there was strictly amateur in keeping with RFU dictates, several of the Japanese teams now represented companies with increasing remuneration obscurity.

Still, that was not yet Tokkie's problem and his accounts were increasing. He was using rugby connections to the full and he was finding business went well with rugger.

Tragedy struck. Tokkie was suddenly thrown into mourning. He was as at heart a sentimental and soft-hearted person who could be easily brought to tears. There were plenty of those in the months ahead.

He and Dilys had a particularly close relationship with Kim Robertson. Then early in 1963 the universally popular Colony captain was gone. After a good party on a visiting ship, he had returned to the Bank residence on The Peak and apparently had fallen by accident from a high window to his death.

Tokkie was inconsolable and looking back at the games, wondering if he and the team should have protected him more and at least been aware of his likely head injuries? This was long before concussion was understood or treated seriously.

After the St John's Cathedral funeral, they all repaired shaken to a popular bar to drink his health accompanied by Bill Riach, a well-liked regular in the Police team.

Two weeks later they were back in the same bar shocked to be drinking to Bill's memory. He had just become engaged and had been celebrating way too much. On the way home, in the New Territories, his ran his car off the road and he did not survive the head injury.

Later in the year the always happy Club and Colony winger Jack Kelly also was killed in a car accident when he drove his sports car off an overpass. Kim, Jack and Tokkie had all played together for Hong Kong against Paris University.

These incidents were all to a large degree alcohol related; everyone certainly did put it back. No one ever worried about heavy drink-

In the news ... Tokkie gets known.

ing and driving; in fact it was the way of life. Intervention by the hands-off colonial police was non-existent. Tokkie often had a hazy memory of the previous evening's end and needed to check his car in the morning. This was also way before seat belts were invented.

A war had broken out in Sarawak and SE Asia, with soldiers actually shooting at each other, so the military took it all a bit more seriously and cut back on some tours.

Tokkie was still Club skipper and pleased to have won the Blarney Stone Sevens Shield, but the fun had gone out of things for a while.

10

Goodbye White Rugby

AT THE end of that season, Frizzles, by then an enthusiastic Hong Kong supporter, sent an excited cable. He had arranged for chairman of NZRFU Tom Morrison and Charlie Saxton, both former All Blacks, to drop in to discuss a possible team stopover on their way to the United Kingdom the coming autumn.

The committee entertained them royally, taking them to the Football Stadium Club and Club bar – naturally – and the new luxury hotels they could now show off. The Kiwis confirmed a short stopover was possible in October but definitely no game due to injury concerns.

Then, out of the blue, another cable was received this time from Taipei University advising the Union they were sending their team to Hong Kong by sea in few weeks. An all-Chinese team again!

The season was technically over, but Tokkie was again pressed into service to mobilise teams and games.

There were somewhat dramatic political differences and shouting going on between Taiwan and the China mainland. Because they were aware of Hong Kong's sensitivity to the issue, the Taiwanese had elected to just turn up!

The team landed from a small steamer in April and they all marched off in line waving a Nationalist flag. A worried-looking

Again in the limelight.

Tokkie was caught standing in the midst of the banners welcoming the visitors, as the excited hoard of pressmen flashed their cameras. He was learning the hazards of international dealings.

Actually, there was no incident but it sure was reassuring to have the Police Commissioner George Wright-Nooth still as chair.

This was of course an unrated team. Chinese guys? The first game was with the Club Dragons to try them out. Playing all their reserves, Taiwan excelled and beat the Dragons easily on a very hard Happy Valley pitch which assisted their open style of game.

Tokkie was shocked and decided he had to put out the full Club selection, which then struggled to hold the visitors' first team to a low-scoring draw.

Political concerns soon evaporated and the Chinese visitors became great friends, singing along in the bar. Their interpreter's translation of the ribald song lines had them doubled up in laughter. Tokkie reveled in all the friendships created.

Their delivery back to the steamer was more relaxed than their arrival and accompanied by backslapping and shouts of goodbye.

They were followed by a sound and much more formal Japanese

CREATING THE HONG KONG SEVENS

Taipei University and Club players formed close relationships.

touring side early the next season. Tokkie was learning the quality of play and enthusiasm for the game being played around him in Asia.

The old days of all-white rugby supremacy were long gone from his mind.

That year, the Union AGM upstairs at the Club had an unusual overflow attendance. Tokkie was by now the Club representative. The RFU had delivered on a stopover by renowned rugby journalist and Welsh star Vivian Jenkins and RFU past president John Tennant.

The large audience, starved of rugby news from back home and of the England tour of Australia and New Zealand, hung on every word. Tokkie had a few drinks with Vivian and had now linked into *The Sunday Times'* top rugby journalist.

The meeting was told it was by no means certain the All Blacks would make a stop in minor Hong Kong. Vivian and John attended a special meeting of the committee which practically begged them to encourage an All Blacks stopover.

Next day the rugger enthusiast New Zealand Trade Commissioner Phil Costello and Government House got in the act, applied political pressure and the telegrams rushed back and forth.

Eventually the news: they are coming!

11

The All Blacks

THE All Blacks' visit was brief but very significant. Finally, just for a moment the entire rugby world was focused on Hong Kong

They arrived October 1963 on the first stop of an ambitious tour. They were to play in the United Kingdom, Ireland, France and Canada; 36 games as it turned out with only one loss.

Their large entourage arrived at daybreak at Kai Tak Airport, all decked out in their team blazers and clearly psyched up. With growing influence, the Union committee took the touring group directly from the plane to a launch next to the runway, shepherded by a beaming Tokkie.

Then, on a beautiful early morning they clearly enjoyed the sparkling voyage across the harbour to the island. The launch docked near the Star Ferry, then just a short walk to the brand new Mandarin Hotel.

They had only agreed to a public training session that evening at the Football Club. The HKRFU treated it like a big game and milked it to maximum extent with advertisements and printed programme.

Tokkie played in the opener: The President's XV against HMNZS *Otago*, which had been brought into port especially for the game. Forget whatever war we are supposed to be fighting, these are our All Blacks!

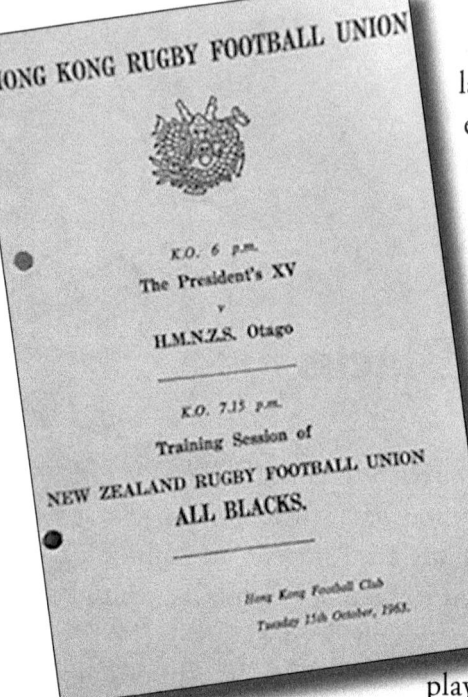

The All Blacks attracted the largest crowd so far seen at a rugby event, some 5000 fans. They were disappointed there was no game but fascinated by the commentary on the training session and players, kindly provided by Kiwi journalists travelling with the team.

Just to watch internationally famous 'The Boot' Don Clarke practising his kicking, Colin Meads marshalling his forwards, or Kevin Briscoe getting his backs running was enough!

Their manager Frank Kilby was apologetic they could not play but thank heavens they did not. The Colony would have been slaughtered. Their short visit did put Hong Kong on the serious international rugby map.

The mighty All Blacks were pictured around the world in the Football Club stadium. They actually have a stadium! Hong Kong rugby had arrived.

The national Thailand team visit later in the year attracted increasing local interest, but nothing approaching the excitement of the All Blacks. The annual Blarney Stone Sevens, expanding in size and attracting a larger crowd, again closed a wonderful season.

* * *

The Club AGM that followed was a packed affair overflowing the upstairs lounge. Finally Bill Leong's mysteriously stalled membership had to be brought to that meeting.

Although the Club had decided in principle way back in 1960 that membership would no longer be restricted to expatriates, somehow

Triumphant Bill Leong breaks through.

Bill's application for membership kept getting delayed.

Tokkie was leading a determined rugby section which had taken this very seriously. The notice went out: everyone attends. Tokkie jumped up and loudly stated he was prepared to resign over the issue.

The feisty, diehard colonialist, Club president Colonel Hugh Dowbiggin stormed out, brandishing his walking stick and shouting he would not allow Chinese in 'his' club. High drama!

The Colonel was a caricature of the British imperialist. Dapper, stern faced, cheroot in one hand and a gin in the other, he was elected president at the age of 77. The Club was constantly in a financial crisis and needed an establishment, old stock figure like the Colonel as president.

Not surprisingly, he had been born in 1884 and nurtured in colonial Ceylon. Not many knew his first name, but everyone addressed him as Colonel.

Bill, on the other hand was an absolutely charming local oil executive, English educated with a posh accent, and a very tough scrum half. The situation was quite ridiculous. Good natured and patient as always, Bill was cheered as he bought his first official round at the packed Men's Bar.

The drama was all behind them when they donned their black ties for the annual Football Club dinner dance at the grand old Repulse Bay Hotel. Tokkie and Dilys, by then in their 30s, were all dressed up and sitting with the Leongs and a new decade of players and newcomers.

The Colonel ... Hugh Dowbiggin.

Young Glen Docherty, later a revered chairman and very senior member of the elite, had made his appearance and was also at their table. At that time he looked up to Tokkie as a local rugger god. Glen later proved a true friend when Tokkie had hit the bottom.

Take that, Colonel! Bill is elected Dragons captain.

Tokkie's eyes were opened again to Asian rugby when in December 1964 he joined a Club touring side to Thailand and Malaysia in support of his great buddy Denny Johnston who had made it to Club captain

He was amazed to find how popular the game was in Thailand where the Club was narrowly beaten by the National team before a packed and noisy stadium.

A further loss to Selangor State, then on to a different experience deep in the jungle at the Malacca army base for a tight loss to the powerful New Zealand Regiment, followed by a riotous beer-up in the huts. They did enjoy hotel luxury in Singapore, drinks at Raffles and different cultured entertainment in that Asian society for two more games, with the new responsible older statesman Tokkie encouraging restrained behaviour.

He was also trying to be respectable because he was always looking for business and Singapore was becoming a key trading and shipping city.

More important for rugby future, they had talks at the grand old Cricket Club about more tours throughout Asia and setting up a more formal system. They were making friends with the local Asian rugger enthusiasts who were beginning to take over the game from the expatriates.

12

The Need for Sponsors

THERE was no rush of teams to the Colony after the All Blacks and the next visitor from outside the region again came from New Zealand, almost a year later in January 1965.

Although international travel was increasing dramatically in volume, the costs were as well. Taking a full rugby team on tour with all its management and hangers-on was a very expensive venture, increasingly being financed in some way by sponsors or business interests.

In the first week of January 1965 finally someone followed up on the All Blacks. The low-budget Canterbury University side arrived and saw a fussed Tokkie and teammates at the Yacht Club parcelling the visitors out to home hosting.

The overwhelming logistics of large group tours were beginning to dawn on him. Especially a wild bunch like this!

They had been in Japan playing six of their best teams and had lost only one game. Now they preceded to beat the President's Selection and then Tokkie's Colony side by two points.

That they did so was a small wonder and a tribute to youth. Their harassed management and the local committee had spent the night, literally, trying to find their key players and extract them from the depths of Wanchai for a few hours' sleep before the game.

The entire rugby community had been pulled in to accommodate

Canterbury set the scene for their win.

and entertain the visitors. Tokkie and many others worked day and night looking after them (and for them) while they were in town.

It all climaxed on their last evening when they had been generously invited to the black tie late Christmas party at the Bank Mess.

A group of their playful team, featuring the Maoris, caused a fun scandal by bringing the tarted-up Wanchai bar girls they had spent their time with as their escorts. Those ladies proved too well known for comfort!

Tokkie and several others literally spent much of the night rounding up the visitors and getting them at sunrise to the big waterfront launch arranged for their delivery across the harbour to Kai Tak Airport.

And there was a slightly teary Tokkie waving his usual emotional goodbye. Or could it have been relief and exhaustion? He was possibly already thinking that next time, arranging sevens preferably with a sponsor might be easier!

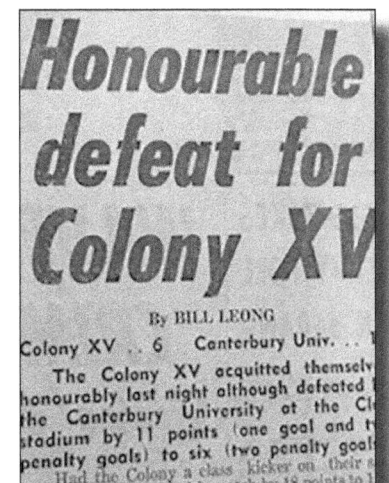

OPENING UP THE GAME!

Part 3

Uniting Asia

Blarney Stone for Tokkie and captain Glen Docherty.

13

Joining the Establishment

BY THE mid-'60s Tokkie had formally joined the administration when he moved on to the HKRFU committee as the Club representative. Significantly, Vernon Roberts who had always been involved, was elected chairman of the Union in 1963. Yes, that Vernon who had welcomed Tokkie at the Gloucester Hotel bar in the first place.

Vernon was enjoying a remarkable rise in his fortunes. He had been appointed manager of the mighty Hongkong Land Company, taking one of the most prestigious positions in the colony. He became an important influence throwing the considerable resources of the large property group behind local rugby.

With increasing ease of travel, prominent international rugby personalities now just turned up. Vernon and Tokkie were in their element formally representing the Union and talking international rugger policy.

Tokkie knew so many Kiwi and Aussie players he was dropping names liberally. His move from the Club to the Union would become significant because he was now building up personal relationships with leaders in international rugby.

He also was starting to demonstrate a more responsible attitude to life and while still for the hard game, started campaigning against dangerous play. He certainly had been proved right about overzealous tackling by Aussie and Kiwi teams. Serious concussions, broken limbs and hospitalisation were common.

Jeremy Wilson had played in the Colony and Club teams for several years and he was considered one of the finest running backs the colony had seen. He never played again after a vicious scissor late tackle by two Kiwi naval visiting players at the Club stadium which caused multiple fractures. Jeremy was hospitalised with extensive injury which resulted in his return to the United Kingdom and a painful struggle initially even to learn to walk again. Tokkie took the incident very personally and provided a close and sympathetic support to Jeremy during his recovery. Later he helped him find a new job in London which resulted in his return to Hong Kong and their families continuing a close friendship.

Tokkie saw this happen and was convinced it was premeditated. He stormed in protest but of course the damage was done.

He was surely becoming more serious; some were saying more pompous.

At a formal rugger dance his close friends Trevor and Shirley Bedford got into an uncharacteristic argument. It got serious on the drive home up The Peak in a storm. Ever determined to make her point Shirley jumped out of the car and in long dress and heels, stomped home up the long hill, soaked through and refusing lifts.

Next morning Tokkie was furious with Trevor dressing him down publicly for his lack of chivalry. Trevor and Shirley had quickly reconciled and thought it a hoot. Tokkie continued lecturing about standards of behaviour.

Trevor, however, had his turn. On a Club tour to Bangkok, around that time, the hosts had thoughtfully arranged Thai massages to work out the stiffness resulting from the truly tough games.

Locating Tokkie's booth, Trevor found benches and brought the team to clamber up and quietly watch over the top. Then at

Chairman Roberts and Hon. Sec. D'Eathe.

an appropriate time they all applauded. Tokkie was absolutely livid and sulked for days. His dignity had been shattered and his authority challenged. It was a long time before he could even chuckle about it.

He was taken very seriously however and respected when he came down heavily on team members who smashed up the Club lounge during a drunken 'Wreck Wi'em Mess' combined bachelor party. Following a deplorable custom then condoned in privileged rugby circles back England, the revelers left the upstairs lounge in ruins, with broken plates and glasses, wrecked furniture and all the large decorative flower pots smashed on the floor.

It was a big party with many of the playing rugger crowd invited. He was there but things got out of hand too quickly for him to intervene.

Such behaviour was alien to the conservatively raised Tokkie and he was absolutely appalled. He identified the culprits publicly, demanded each gave the Club a personal apology and assessed them with the costs of repair.

He certainly was moving up in status and increasingly his relationship with Vernon Roberts was beginning to dominate his life.

It is impossible to do justice briefly to Vernon's amazing personally

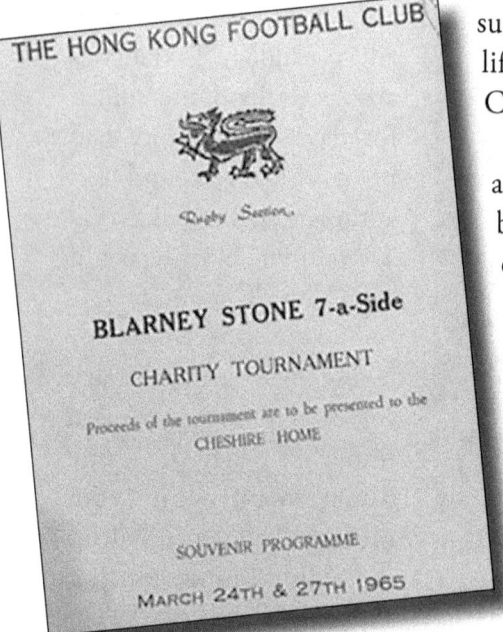

successful, cavalier and hedonistic life. Perhaps one of the last true China Coast Hands.

The ebullient Vernon and his attractive and warm wife Linda, both partied hard, which apparently was related to her tragic death. They had befriended Tokkie and Dilys and taken them into their circle from the time of their arrival.

When Tokkie originally met him at the Gloucester Hotel, Vernon had not been his usual forceful and bustling self but underweight and lethargic. He was still recovering from a serious thrombosis in his leg suffered during a squash game a couple of years before.

He had been a dashing fly-half and recovered enough to struggle out occasionally for the 'Old and Bold' team, heavily bandaged.

Against all odds, by sheer power of personality, he had taken over management of the land company, the venerable owner of most of the Central District office buildings. With no formal business training he had moved from overseeing that small Gloucester Hotel to controlling a developing real estate empire.

Now, he was brimming with self-confidence earned by his leadership and flair in conceiving and building the first magnificent Mandarin Hotel. His entry into rugby administration added official recognition of the increasing business value of rugby.

Rugby was also gaining in influence, as Tokkie found when the question had arisen how the Union could afford to accommodate the All Blacks' contingent of 50 if they came? Vernon had shrugged and said, "We will put them in the Mandarin", immediately seeing an international public relations coup.

He spent a couple of years in the middle 1960s as chairman of the HKRFU but he liked to be the 'boss man' and moved to President of the Union in 1966 through to his death in 1977.

He founded the Asian RFU in 1969 and significantly a few years later he was President and Tokkie was Chairman of HKRFU, when the Sevens were developed from a wild idea through to a working reality.

Vernon was also distinguished President of the Football Club from 1968 until 1977 when high living finally caught up with him. To add to his mystique during that time he started sporting a monocle and exaggerating his army officer accent. All in big business and real life!

Appearances were also changing for Tokkie, whose scratched glass beer mug and shared peanuts at the Football Club Bar was now often replaced by an overflowing chilled silver tankard and canapés at the Captain's Bar in the Mandarin Hotel.

14

Last of the Amateur Toffs

BY THE mid-1960s tourism had become an important industry for Hong Kong with never-ending planes roaring low over the peninsula rooftops into Kai Tak.

Locals were increasingly away from the colony as business expanded in Asia and visits to Europe, Australia and North America had become more frequent. The amazing Xerox made communication instantaneous.

Everything was speeding up. The norm for colonialists had been three- to five-year tours with a six-month 'home' leave. Most enjoyed contracts with generous provident funds calculated for a retirement at 55. No such luck for Tokkie who would have to provide his own pension.

The increasing casualness of travel did allow for more visits to the UK. Tokkie found with a bit of cunning these could be timed to coincide with a big game at Twickenham where friends like Frizzles and John Tallent could lavishly return the entertainment they had received in Hong Kong.

The mid-1960s also brought the inconsiderate buildup of US naval and military presence in Vietnam which totally screwed up the Vietnamese rugger schedules and prevented tours. US recreation was to prove a bonanza for the girls in Wanchai, however, although it drove up their prices; and beer prices too.

※ ※ ※

Early in 1966, back from a Club tour of Japan organised with friend Shiggy Konno, Tokkie found himself pitched full time for days into helping to arrange a rugby festival, naturally under the instructions of Vernon.

The committee had relatively short time to plan but brought Japanese and Taiwanese teams to Hong Kong for a British Festival Week. This was his first experience of formally planning an international rugby tournament, and he loved it.

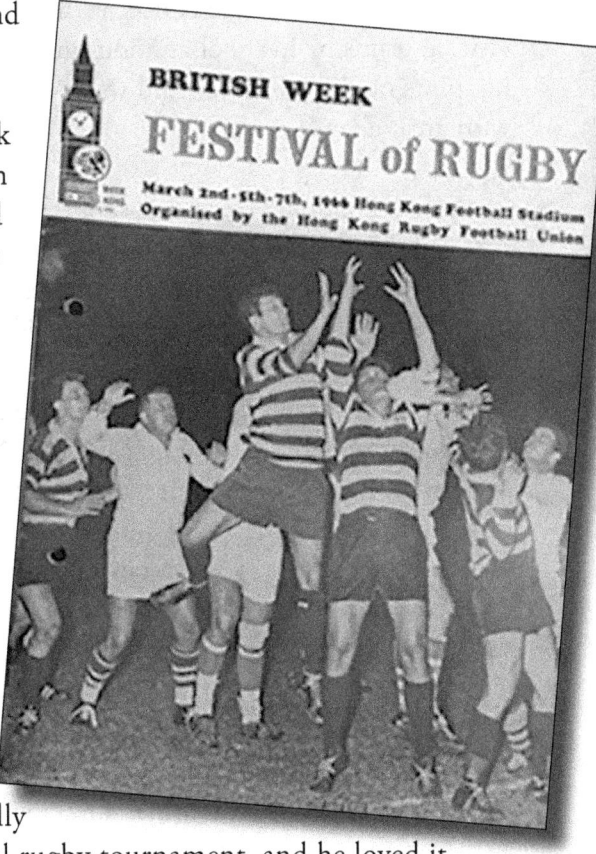

The festival, graced by Princess Margaret and Tony Snowden in March, was presented with much fanfare. Vernon greeted the royal couple at the new Princes Building and escorted them proudly across the just-opened footbridge to the Mandarin.

It was a well-publicised rugby festival, complete with lavish programmes, and was the first rugger event to attract a local Chinese crowd, drawn by the publicised visiting Asian players. The Club beat the Japanese Combined Universities Acorns and Taiwan in close games.

CREATING THE HONG KONG SEVENS

The Japanese beat the Police. Vernon threw a lavish party for the visiting teams by his pool at Shouson Hill. It was a wild affair serving pints of chilled Scotch and water the visitors loved and downed with great abandon.

Back in London, Frizzles had spoken to one of the biggest names in UK rugby, Bill Ramsay. The jovial Bill W. C. Ramsay, was an England RFU past president. Frizzles had interested him in what was going on in Hong Kong and Bill decided to visit.

Tipped off by Frizzles that Bill was of enormous influence at RFU, Vernon and the committee decided to go all out to impress him.

The committee met Bill and his wife Nora at Kai Tak and took them by private boat to their grand suite at the Mandarin. A bottle of Scotch before dinner, (and Nora could match Bill drink for drink), set them up well to stagger upstairs to an informal but typically lavish dinner with Vernon at the Button restaurant on the hotel roof patio, sitting by the sparkling mosaic Casadei-designed swimming pool.

Bill said he liked to be one of 'the lads', so Tokkie spent the next morning seriously hung over and ordering up a crowd of players for lunch in the bar at the Hong Kong Club.

Vernon had planned a formal dinner with the ladies later, way out at his estate on Shouson Hill. A typhoon blew up and the number seven signal instructed 'Stay at home!'

At Bill's insistence they drove through the typhoon for drinks by Vernon's enormous fireplace, to a background of howling wind. Then a gourmet dinner supported by special bottles from Vernon's impressive cellar, and a wild struggle back through the level eight storm.

After that they called him "Typhoon" Ramsay and it became Bill's big Hong Kong story. He met the committee formally to discuss Hong Kong's growing rugby significance and Tokkie now had an important inside contact at Twickenham.

They were nevertheless very aware that times were changing and

Bedford, now captain, and Tokkie follows.

that Bill would be one of the last old toffs of RFU who had controlled rugby from its beginning. Their power was diminishing like that of the Empire.

Tokkie made even more significant practical friendships when the Australian establishment Wallaroos came to play the Colony in 1967. By now Trevor Bedford was captain. Tokkie still barely held on to his selection in the second row. A decade later he would be inviting his Wallaroo friends to the first Hong Kong Sevens and cheering them on in the final!

15

Family Affairs

TOKKIE'S much younger sister Beth arrived in Hong Kong in the mid-'60s from England and soon was seen at stylish fashion shows with Dilys. She decided to stay on with them at their smart apartment at Repulse Bay, overlooking the beach.

An incident involving the youthful Beth happened which showed a perplexing other side to Tokkie's character. His sister, a beautiful, super-fit young woman not long graduated from National Ballet School in London, had just found exciting employment as a manager of Hong Kong's first discotheque in the Peninsula Hotel.

Tokkie heard from friends they had seen her holding hands on a beach with a young Indian fellow whom he had not met but who lived nearby. He flew into a rage and angrily forbad her to see him again. Typically, he would hear no explanation and their argument was so violent she threw clothes into her bag, stormed out and left.

He was later terribly upset by the confrontation and got hell from his wife. He asked himself whether he was just trying to assert his authority. Was he genuinely thinking to protecting his little sister or was it a racist reaction? Perhaps he had just not taken the time to get to know him?

Beth never returned. She left essentially penniless but like her mother before her, she proved totally independent. She settled suc-

Tokkie's sister Beth.

cessfully in Hong Kong and on her own initiative enjoyed a very successful career.

Tokkie had arrived in Hong Kong married, surrounded at the Club mainly by bachelors. So it did not concern him directly but he was aware inter-racial marriage was still very much frowned upon by the colonialists, although nowhere nearly as bitterly as in South Africa.

During a first tour of up to five years a new arrival contracted not to marry without company approval. It was understood this approval would not be forthcoming if it involved inter-racial marriage. In fact, he knew a young fellow had been recently sent home by a big company for getting too involved with a Chinese woman.

The British Empire had been built upon maintaining ruling-class purity.

Things were progressively getting more liberal. His referee friend, who was later to be a power in Colony rugby, was married to a beautiful and talented Asian woman. Being an independent doctor he could do what the hell he wanted.

They gave a dinner party and the somewhat inebriated male guests stupidly made inappropriate remarks. She was tolerant enough, but she really did not appreciate some of the cruder 'male' humour. In self-defence she developed her own brand.

At the end of the meal she said, polite as ever but in her best pidgin English, "*Ellyone fuckoffee!*"

* * *

As the decade drew to a close, Tokkie's personal life had been unravelling. He and Dilys abruptly spit up. Unknown to her, he had developed something of a lady's man reputation of which his close friends at the Men's Bar were well aware.

Females, of course, had a reputation for gossip but the Men's Bar buzzed with the latest on the 'hot birds' who had arrived in the colony. The bachelors maintained the coveted 'party list' of single women available for the series of parties given at the bachelor residences.

Discourteously, but inevitably, those listed tended to get discussed and the ladies were rated around the bar.

Across town, the girls had fun with their own reporting system. A corresponding men's party list was maintained and evaluated far more frankly and critically by the young ladies at the Helena May Institute, the local 'virgins' retreat' on Garden Road.

Notwithstanding the scrutiny, unions satisfactory to both lists were frequently made. Although he attempted to be discrete, after a few beers it became evident Tokkie's contributions to the evaluation process at the bar seemed only to have come from firsthand knowledge.

Not that anyone had a reason to get himself involved in a complicated personal social problem if he was only looking for a little action.

An overwhelming number of women seeking employment had flowed into Hong Kong from China and many of these were actively employed in the entertainment and sex trade of Tsim Sha Tsui and Wanchai, as glorified by the colourful world of Suzie Wong.

A great advantage was that these streets were all safe for business and clients at night due, it was rumoured, to the excellent service provided by those Five Dragons who controlled the back rooms of the police force in cahoots with the Triads that had been forced out of China. Naturally the amount of money available dictated the quality of service the ladies provided.

It was the normal practice for Chinese entrepreneurs to offer alluring company at business dinners and Tokkie, among many others, found himself constantly fighting off that temptation. Many of them maintained apartments especially designed to have parties and entertain business guests. The particularly imaginative hosts also brought in girls from Europe, Australia and other countries.

They seemed happy together.

Away on business in any part of Asia, Tokkie had as tactfully as possible to resist the women that business contacts always pushed but the amount of alcohol they all drank unfortunately tended to reduce resistance!

Then there were those very smart afternoon tea dance salons, tucked away discretely, especially supported by local Chinese gentlemen. These were used for business entertainment and providing shapely and beautifully gowned women offering dance cards, who were available for small talk, to discuss more interesting personal activities or even infrequently to dance.

The volume trade was satisfied by the notorious bar girls who were tough little ladies accustomed to negotiating their short time or long time fees with American sailors and servicemen. Plus of course the

CREATING THE HONG KONG SEVENS

Bars mainly for fun and to drink gallons of beer in the heat.

bar buyout payment mentioned later to be agreed with the barman. This activity she repeated several times each night!

It was into this rough but exciting area of Wanchai that the Men's Bar would empty late in the evening on special occasions with the cry of "Exhibish!"

Hong Kong was a curious Victorian place which frowned on any of these sex-driven activities officially or in public. Even nudity was banned from nightclubs and shows. The new risqué *Playboy* magazine, which had brazenly moved beyond bare breasts, was hidden on the bookstore back shelves wrapped in brown paper.

This was long before the days of free pornography and sexually explicit material. Grainy black-and-white sex movies were shown in the depths of the red light districts, down back alleys and in crowded, smoky and stifling rooms.

The so-called exhibitions were usually staged, by quiet arrangement, in a corner suite of one of the Wanchai short-time hotels. A bar was run in the corridor by the room boy and local star performers attempted to disrobe artistically to scratchy phonograph music and perform satisfactorily surrounded by a noisy but encouraging audience.

On one memorable rugger occasion, after such a party, following the Blarney Stone Sevens, Tokkie had to return in the cold of the early morning to help search for a just-won silver tankard, misplaced somehow in the confusion as the show climaxed.

Wanchai was for most players really just a lot of fun. Although they all knew the girls by name, visiting the bars was mainly to enjoy the atmosphere, make a lot of noise with pals and drink gallons of San Mig beer, while dripping sweat in the heat.

But there was no escape. Even Tokkie's monthly barber got into the act, offering back-room, comforting massages to smooth away his business worries.

That was all that was going on until Terry came into his life. She was far removed from these occasional indiscretions and was mature, poised and very attractive. Like Dilys before her she literally swept Tokkie off his feet.

This all came about as part of a traumatic change in his business life. Up to 1967, Tokkie's relationship with Stockland and Ferguson had expanded very successfully particularly with respect to the Dunhill business which in Asia now represented a large slice of their international sales.

This drew the attention of the powerful Jardine company who seduced them away from Tokkie and formed a partnership.

The new partnership took over not only the tobacco business but all of his textile clients except Pringle.

He had shares in Stockland and Ferguson but they offered him the position of Far East Managing Director in lieu of the share value. He insisted he had the right to both and the fractious dispute resulted in him being paid off and over his protestations marched out of the building by security.

A positive result had been that during failing negotiations in London in 1967 he had met Terry Smith, interestingly with the same surname. An attractive, beautifully dressed and engaging businesswoman she was the senior knitwear buyer at Harrods fashions in London.

She was quite a bit older than Tokkie and married with a grown family. He seemed to like older women and was quickly head over heels in love with her. Colleagues joked he talked about her constantly and could not wait to get back to her at Harrods every evening.

Their hot relationship continued upon his return to Hong Kong and developed during frequent 'necessary' business trips to Europe.

After a lot of quiet scheming, a couple of years later Terry moved to Hong Kong, and upon her arrival she quickly replaced Dilys. Tokkie already had ADC Smith and Co. operating and she also joined the

Terry.

company adding considerable flair and expertise to the management. They immediately started expanding the business.

All the sympathy was with Dil! For a while he was an outcast, until they too were beguiled by Terry's easy charm. Some friendships, however, never quite recovered and Tokkie's reputation took a hard hit.

Their break-up was absolutely unexpected by Dilys. She had been working for Vernon as his personal and confidential assistant for several years demonstrating the closeness of the rugby establishment.

By that time Vernon had remarried the stunningly beautiful and blonde, younger Bonnie from California, as was expected of him.

Dilys herself was soon remarried to a charming auto agency millionaire in their group and moved to the upscale beachside village of Shek-O. Such was the closeness of their society and of the rugby set they were soon all seen out politely chatting at functions together.

16

The Roberts Era

VERNON Roberts had started his significant 10-year presidency of HKRFU in 1966. Tokkie was slowing down on the field and, signalling the end of his playing career, the Football Club made him a life member for leadership service to rugby and after 21 Colony caps, captaining 12 games. He had toured Saigon, Thailand Singapore Malaysia and Japan.

It was a time of great expansion in the game during the late '60s and Vernon, Tokkie and colleagues were moving Hong Kong into the international rugby scene. Back home the antiquated toffs like Frizzles and Typhoon Ramsay continued struggling to keep RFU internationally relevant and in control.

The last thing they wanted was new ideas or changes to their traditional concept of their gentlemen's game. Their function was to protect and strengthen the status quo.

The '60s, however, produced an almost universal questioning of authority and development of new ideas. Rugby was moving towards a more competitive, open and spectator-pleasing game. This raised the spectre of an end to the amateur game with professionalism and, horrors, big money in the sport.

None of this particularly crossed Tokkie's mind as he became more involved in rugby management nor was it really relevant to the local scene. However, the politics of international rugby and what was going on in England was about to have an enormous impact on his own life.

There had been a continuing reduction in the number of countries and territories controlled by the British Empire with a further two dozen leaving during the '60s.

However, the more immediate thing for him was going on in Asia, where he and a team of friends, Glen Docherty, Tommy Roberts, Trevor Bedford, Denny Johnston and others were working under Vernon's eagle eye, intent on setting up an Asian rugby association.

Vernon Roberts.

Achieving that became the most important regional rugby focus of the closing decade. It was also a highly significant step towards inclusiveness in international rugby.

In 1968, to Vernon's great satisfaction, the Asian Rugby Football Union was founded. This was followed in 1969 by the inaugural Asian Rugby Football Tournament in Tokyo.

The tournament featured Thailand, South Korea, Taiwan, plus Japan beating Hong Kong by two points in a hard-fought final game to the enormous pleasure of the organiser and their drinking buddy Shiggy Konno.

They had now joined in uniting a large network of Asian rugger enthusiasts and had set the scene for Hong Kong to emerge as their international focus point. Sunshine rugger was on the way!

Tokkie, meanwhile, had been rebuilding his business shattered by the loss of Dunhill and Stockland and Ferguson to Jardine. He had a further setback when Pringle also left to set up their own office.

Asia holds first ever international multi-racial rugby tournament

Working now with Terry, who was an extremely capable businesswoman, and investing the cash from the Stockland and Ferguson share sale they had set up their new business as ADC Smith and Co. in the prestigious Star House near the ferry in Kowloon.

Not withstanding the loss of his two main clients, with the surge in Hong Kong business at the time and the help of the very bright Terry, he build a successful business such to set themselves up in a fine house on Wilson Road in the prestigious Jardine Lookout and to rent a smart apartment in Chelsea.

17

Finally, England

AT THE beginning of the 1970s the vast majority of people in Hong Kong had never even heard of rugby let alone the RFU of England. In contrast, Singapore had introduced rugby as a required sport in the schools producing a generation of local players.

In Hong Kong it remained a strange game played with an odd ball by the colonials, tucked away in the Happy Valley club. The Macanese were more educated on account of the occasional Macau tour.

From time to time, someone organised a tour to Macau. Two teams were selected and they set off partying by ferry across the delta to the Portuguese gambling city, complete with a swinging band of followers.

They were going to play against themselves but this did not lessen the rivalry that developed. The game itself was livened up by the large crowd of locals who always gathered to watch the remarkable spectacle of shouting white "English" fellows violently embracing and knocking each other down, blowing whistles and chasing a strangely shaped ball that was designed not to bounce in a straight line.

Plus, like all proverbial mad dogs, they ran out in the midday sun.

The weekend, as expected, was a riot of fun with gambling, dancing to the excellent Filipino bands and endless exotic cocktails.

It became a sought after selection and an awaited and never-ending source of mirth for the Macanese.

The Stadium now hosted the best ever Blarney Stone Sevens, which by 1970 had become a three-day tournament. This 32-team festival of rugby was now the gala rugby event of the year. Even so, a small part of the stands accommodated the crowd of expatriates who turned up annually to watch, jeer, cheer and drink beer with enthusiasm and generally have a good time.

That other competitive Sevens tournament was about to develop locally, but even so the Shield games survived until the end of the 1980s.

The year 1971 was the 100th anniversary of RFU, and to great excitement the England team, boasting 120 caps, finally came to Hong Kong in September. Their extensive Asian tour dropped them off in Hong Kong after Japan for a quick game. Remarkably, the game was tied at halftime and Hong Kong lost by a respectable score.

Typhoon Ramsay had played no small part in getting the team to stop in Hong Kong, so that hangover

England at the Football Club stadium.

from the Mandarin party had paid off. Bill had been RFU chairman from Middlesex way back in 1954. He had been brought back in to serve as chairman again for the centennial year, after years of manoeuvring, he joked, and this had won him a knighthood.

Now, when they phoned he insisted, "Cut out the Sir William crap", although secretly he loved it. "But forget Lady Nora at your peril!"

Vernon, Tokkie and the Hong Kong Union had scored a coup just getting them there but the good personal relationships formed were not to remain cordial in the early Sevens years ahead.

By 1972 the harbour waterfront reclamation had been finished and work was underway on the cross-harbour tunnel. That period also signalled the China Awakening and heralded an unprecedented stock market and property boom. United States President Richard Nixon visited China. Hong Kong was now a commercial centre and an international tourist destination. Tokkie and everyone prospered and the good times looked like they would never end.

But all was not totally well. He and dejected fellow beer drinkers found themselves at the Football Club bar surrounded by smirking women drinking cocktails.

Their exclusive Men's Bar retreat was gone; the choir silenced. Everyone knew China was coming one day, but this truly signalled the end of the Empire!

The profits continued to roll in, which was why they were there! The British Empire had been created not by governments but by corporations and traders out to make money.

Hong Kong was doing well carrying on that tradition. Tokkie and Terry found that in their personal life almost everything they did was dominated by business. Social relationships tended to be very shallow and close friendships were rare.

Life was urbane, intense and objective. There were endless cocktail parties, functions, office promotions, fashion shows, balls and charity events.

Then the excellent restaurants, night clubs, and bars to frequent and be seen in. They had to belong to the right clubs, accumulating expensive memberships.

They struggled to appear at the social events demanded at the Hong Kong Club, the Cricket Club, the Yacht Club, the Jockey Club and, of course, the Football Club. It was all becoming a continuous entertainment blur, drink in hand.

Dinner parties at home and the popular Sunday curry lunches were more personal but still good for business discussion.

> **This lack of genuine friendship would reveal itself later when Tokkie ran into trouble.**

The weekend could not be easily wasted on pleasure and launch trips were almost always business based. Golf was to spend time with the right people and of course later Tokkie just had to play at that incredibly expensive club.

They found it quite normal to have friends they spoke to every day but with whom they never discussed anything really profound. This lack of genuine friendship would reveal itself later when Tokkie ran into trouble. One sound friend continued to be Vernon, although he now expected to be addressed as Mr Roberts by all except his close friends.

A stoutish figure, he affected that monocle screwed menacingly in his eye and projecting his confident take-charge personality, not only on the rugby scene. At the government land auction he outbid everyone, famously photographed just keeping his hand up, to secure the land for Connaught Centre (later Jardine House) at a world record price.

Tokkie was approaching 40, not playing but still in fair shape.

Tokkie and Terry party with Richard Dunhill.

He was very much the busy travelling businessman with his trading and rugby interests comfortably intermingled. He was active in ADC Smith and Co. investing in the stock market like everyone else, prospering and living very happily with Terry, whom for some reason, he seems never to have actually married.

All his social life revolved around his original rugger pals who were beginning to dominate local business. Most prominent was Vernon, President of the HKRFU since 1967, and now clearly rugby's top man.

18

Tokkie Takes Over

WAY back in their carefree young days, his Club rugger crowd congregated every Sunday morning at Big Wave Bay, carting their beer coolers, escorted by bikinied young wives and girlfriends.

The hot day was spent throwing the ball around on the beach, showing off to the ladies and trying to avoid the rocks while body surfing. Then back to the Yacht Club or wherever for dinner.

He and his ageing rugby pals still on occasion made it out to play by the sea at Big Wave Bay but with brief ball action, wives in modest swimsuits and longer periods sitting around the beer cooler.

It was a good example of the close relationship between business and rugby when his long time Scottish client and friend, Willie Mactaggart, chairman of Pringle, asked him personally to bring a Hong Kong team to the Border Sevens.

Willie had been invited to be president of his Hawick RU in their centenary year and they had extended their Easter seven-a-side games in celebration.

The tournament would be held in Scotland where the wee game was invented, over Easter ending on April 21, 1973. Tokkie jumped at the chance. He had always loved Sevens and the Blarney Stone games had become such a popular success in Hong Kong.

The warm weather Blarney Stones ended the 1973 season as usual at the end of March and the Union selected an impressive Colony representative team. As manager, he took them all out for an inspirational team-building training session at Big Wave Beach a few days before they left.

Sand and sunny beaches did not work in damp, dark Scotland and after that long trip, he was depressed when they were eliminated early in biting cold weather, with snow flurries, sleet and then freezing, drenching rain. What did they expect, this was Scotland in April.

He now remembered the difference of playing in this miserable, cold weather compared to his spirit-lifting sunny-weather game in Asia!

At least he had the consolation of beginning Hong Kong's tradition of touring Sevens sides and on their return *The Post* hailed them encouragingly as "rugby ambassadors".

It had turned out to be a disappointing month all round. By chance, that season brought the centenary not only of Hawick but also of the Scottish Rugby Union itself. They had announced the SRU Centenary Sevens Tournament which would be the first ever international Sevens tournament to be held on April 7 at historic Murrayfield.

Tokkie had planned to arrive in time and stay on for the Borders but mounting and continuing business problems had kept him in Hong Kong.

He was bitterly disappointed and the tournament was all over before he arrived. The usual countries had been invited: Scotland, England, Wales, Ireland, Australia, New Zealand and

France plus a Scottish invitation team to replace South Africa, making the eight.

Being South African, he was indignant to learn they had not been invited but he understood the reason: apartheid sanctions.

He was now accustomed to playing regularly with people of many races and it stood out that those who had been invited to Murrayfield were all from the traditional white rugby cultures. He found this somewhat hypocritically in light of the fuss over what was going on in South Africa.

To add insult the Scottish invitation team had fielded three white Springboks. White! Why had they not invited a team from his Asia or some players from the Pacific Islands, he wondered? Here was a wonderful opportunity to open up the game and it had been sadly missed.

Tokkie was generally appalled at the apartheid situation but had not been back to South Africa for years and was not personally involved. It was the reason he had left the country and he strongly opposed the racist division of their game.

But this was a time of very confused values. Before he got too critical he knew he had to admit the deep irony that his Sevens team selected to represent Hong Kong in Scotland had been all expatriate.

Things had to change!

Vernon 'appointed' Tokkie chairman of HKRFU in mid-1973.

By this time the third Asian Rugby Football Tournament had been held in Hong Kong and Tokkie inherited a well-established Asian rugby family. He and Vernon knew everyone, held all the cards, and started to run the Union together.

One of his first happy jobs was to contact pal Shiggy Kommo who had been appointed chair of the Japanese RFU the previous year and was taking the Japanese national team for its first trip to the UK.

Tokkie got on well personally with Vernon. They were both mainly

All expatriate team to represent Hong Kong.

concept people and could pleasantly drink and bullshit together for hours.

They were assisted by a host of enthusiastic supporters all taking part in helping to organise local and Asian rugby, debating issues loudly at the Football or Cricket Club bars or in some other lunchtime hostelry. A summons to the Hong Kong Club or Chinnery Bar meant something serious was afoot! Or now to Vernon's swank Land Company private club atop Princes Building.

This arrangement was fine for big company manager Vernon. He would give orders and dozens of minions ran to obey. Now his minions included Chairman Tokkie, who was being severely hit by the recession and was stretched for time. He also did not take kindly to instructions.

This was 20 years before serious big money took control and the International Rugby Board declared the game a professional sport. Amateur, of course, extended also to the administration of the game, which meant doing it for free and in your spare time.

Tokkie used contacts through the game extensively and that certainly produced business. However, in no way did that compensated for the disproportionate time he was beginning to expend upon the game. He and his colleagues in rugby had no idea what they were taking on.

* * *

There were also occupational hazards. Beer is the life blood of rugby and Tokkie certainly did his bit to uphold that tradition. However the volume was getting to him so he increasingly resorted to the hard stuff. Not that everyone else was not pretty much sozzled late in the evening at the Taipan's game dinner, which indeed was the idea. After all, the Taipan was buying!

It was evident to all that Tokkie was going to have real trouble making the speech thanking the business leader for his largesse.

He made it up onto the table and actually did a pretty fair job under the circumstances encouraged by loud cheers, friendly encouragement and laughter.

However, it was evident he was regularly hitting the bottle too hard. They did not know his father had died young and as an alcoholic. Particularly in business this was a drinking society where entertain-

Terry joins the team in Scotland.

ment was a key component. Even so, his business associates were increasingly warning him about overdoing it.

Trouble was, every night was a Taipan's night to Tokkie and truth to tell for most of the folks around him.

* * *

In 1973 an inevitable stock market downturn came to Hong Kong and started to put considerable strain on business.

Tokkie ran into severe financial problems about then, but he was still spending an enormous amount of his time on rugby matters. Those critical years were to make him and break him.

That market crash devastated ADC Smith and Co. and also left him personally in a difficult financial state from which he never recovered. They were forced to close down their grand office in Star House, move to a small office in Central and seek more modest housing.

Part 4

Founding the Sevens

19

Big Money

TOKKIE'S now quite small and cluttered office looked out on the street from a lower floor window of one of the Central buildings. 1974 had been a terrible year for him financially with the Hong Kong stock market finally bottoming-out in December. Now he was into 1975 and struggling to make a comeback.

He was a charming and convincing salesman but not the tough unscrupulous closer demanded in Asia. His colleagues were concerned that he had made some disastrous business deals. They admitted ruefully that they had all been too far into the stock market.

His business problem stemmed from his self-characterisation as a concepts man, but he was discovering often the devil was indeed in the detail, for which he had little patience.

The positive thing was that rugger was going well. Tokkie had been Union chairman for a couple of years and his business associates told him it was taking up way too much time he could ill afford. He was pleased that the local programmes and the Asian activities were under control and now somewhat routine.

He had joined the Asian Rugby Football council and was taking a Colony team to the Asian games in Korea in April.

The rugby year had opened splendidly on New Year's Day when the fellows at the Club were presented with a major challenge by a

The Hong Kong Club.

beautiful group of new players. They were soundly beaten by the recently formed ladies team although unfairly disconcerted by their quite legal French maid uniforms. This was followed by a final and decisive assault on The Bar, still dominated by men, for mixed-gender, after-game drinks, and a jubilant party.

It would be two decades before women in Hong Kong took up contact rugby seriously, but they had been seen throwing the ball around, which was a start.

More seriously, Tokkie was planning a very special rugby event, the anticipated arrival of the large Welsh national contingent in September.

He could still easily spare the time to take the five-minute walk over to the grand old Hong Kong Club and have another liquid lunch with acquaintance Ian Gow of Rothmans.

The beautiful, mellow heritage building could only later have been demolished by a profit-obsessed society. It was steeped in history and was the prestigious spot in town for a light lunch and a couple of cool drinks on a hot day.

There was no eureka moment when sponsorship and the Sevens idea suddenly occurred to them. Strangely, it all came down to tobacco sales.

From the beginning Tokkie had represented Dunhill products, so he had some commercial overlap and his own tobacco connections in London. He knew many companies around the world were in the market to sponsor rugby.

Sponsorship was not a new idea to anyone on Tokkie's board. In fact it was a hot subject being debated all over the rugger world.

Everyone in rugby administration knew that RFU, far away at Twickenham, thought they were fighting for the very soul of rugby. More and more sponsorships were appearing which told them the sport was heading towards the dreaded professionalism.

At that time tobacco was a vast and highly competitive international industry. Back in England, the already commercial rugby league had stolen a march on the RFU by having John Player not only as sponsor in 1971 but achieve the coveted BBC coverage.

Ian Gow.

※ ※ ※

Tokkie also was aware rugby union in England looked askance at any hint of professionalism or remuneration, but in practice was being forced to turn a blind eye to many such activities.

Sir Bill had moved on but Tokkie was regularly in touch with his other friends at RFU with which he was formally affiliated.

Ian had his bosses from marketing head office in London breathing down his neck. Others in the company later claimed to have initiated the Sevens idea. They suspected John Player had an inside track at Twickenham and were successfully negotiating a first ever sponsorship deal with the Union.

They too needed a rugby sponsorship, and to outdo Imperial Tobacco, their big rival, it must happen by next spring, 1976.

This was purely business. They had suggested to Tokkie that they work with the Hong Kong Union to invite countries to send full national teams to the colony to compete in an international knockout competition, all sponsored and financed by Rothmans.

Big money makes its entry

Ian admitted he was mainly "a lawn bowls fellow" but enjoyed watching the game. His interest was solely in making money for the tobacco industry but he was prepared to pay for everything. That got Tokkie's close attention.

It was then totally socially acceptable to sell tobacco products and Ian was a pillar of the community. Tokkie paused silently, with his brow furrowed, as he did when he was doubtful.

The workload and logistics would be daunting. Bad enough already.

He did eventually convince himself it could work and decided it was just too good a business opportunity to miss.

He first talked to Vernon, of course, and then approached the key people on his board and the

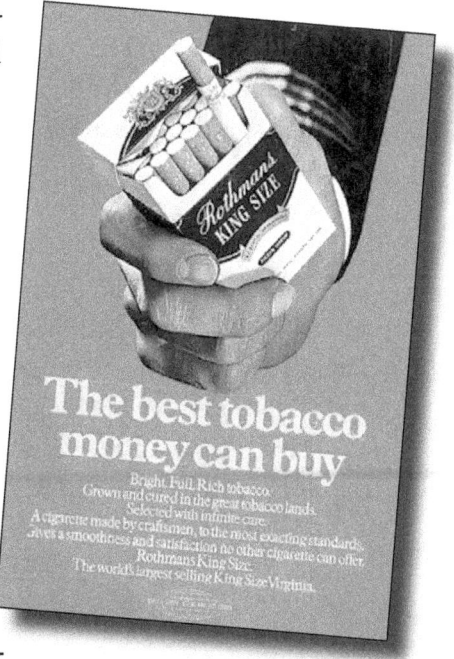

rugger crowd generally to get their reaction.

In this small rugby community, any story got around in a day, and the whole idea of a tournament and sponsorship was debated extensively before it got too far.

Many people would later claim credit for the idea for the Sevens. Tokkie and the Union executive received a great deal of advice!

As the discussion proceeded, Tokkie's passion and arguments for Sevens were winning the day. He had just returned from the Border Sevens. The Blarney Stones had developed into an annually anticipated rugger festival, beloved by all. These were unpredictable games, great fun to watch, and certainly crowd pleasers. And much easier to manage and cheaper to sponsor.

Tokkie's claim to being the founder of the Sevens rests on just that: his determined insistence on a Sevens tournament. Ian and the sponsors demanded the 'big game'. Vernon and the local executive supported Tokkie's push for Sevens.

It was tense but the tobacco company conceded, and they all settled on Sevens. They developed an outline financial proposal with Rothmans, who had learned by then that Imperial Tobacco had indeed snagged the first RFU sponsorship in London for the 1975-76 club competition season and a spring final. The race was on.

Later in the year, long-time rugger player and enthusiast Jock Campbell, now a senior manager at Cathay Pacific, offered to join them as a co-sponsor.

If anyone deserved his rugger elite status, it was Jock. He had played for years, was in the Colony team that toured Japan in 1952 and was a member of the Vernon's original Gloucester Bar crowd.

Jock Campbell.

Now it was a deal they could not refuse!

20

Decision

THE problem was that they were affiliated with the RFU in Twickenham which was part of the 'big boys' International Rugby Football Board.

Over the years Tokkie had built up many connections there but knew his task as chairman to get the approval of this great idea might not be easy. Not that approval was on his mind. When Tokkie decided on something, the details took care of themselves!

Although it was developing a rugby reputation, Hong Kong was a mere colony, far away. It turned out neither the RFU nor the IRFB was about to be rushed or pushed about by upstart Hong Kong.

Maybe next year they could think about it. They had technical reasons for restricting international tournaments, but were secretly worried their own tobacco sponsorship negotiation might be compromised.

History records the colonialists pushed ahead on their own, late in the year, committing to a sponsored Asian Sevens.

Since it could not be an 'international' event they cunningly issued invitations to clubs which they thought neatly got around that problem.

The main question was not so much sponsorship in principle, which RFU was apparently now itself about to accept. It was who

controlled the terms of the sponsorship and could make the deals. More simply, like it or not, money was becoming a big factor in rugby union!

Tokkie turned a blind eye to the fact that RFU had advised him just a couple of years before that they had set up a committee specifically to deal with sponsorships and advise associates how to behave in situations such as this. Tokkie's board had no time for committee nonsense and all those memorandums and details!

He took comfort that the RFU weasel words at the time said that patronage and com-

The Welsh demolish the Colony, but turnout encourages Sevens sponsors.

mercial assistance were acceptable provided they benefitted the game. "Well," he thought, "this sure will benefit ours!"

There were already threats of legal action and reprisals from London which Hong Kong naturally ignored. It took many years and the incredible success of the games for that situation to sort itself out. In fact, it would be 20 years before England sent a national side to the HK Sevens.

In the middle of all this plotting Hong Kong managed to receive and very successfully entertain the team from Wales, then probably the best anywhere. While Hong Kong's side lost by an unmentionable score, it provided highly entertaining rugby and a big turnout which encouraged the still uncommitted Sevens sponsors.

Adding to Tokkie's stress, he took the Colony team to the Asian tournament in Sri Lanka, and they entertained Bangkok at home and played Manila away.

Sponsors start to assert influence

Tokkie knew everyone of significance in the rugby world. At this point in his career the Rolodex on the corner of his desk was already spinning impressively.

He was having a wonderful time with all this rugby, but with bigger money now at stake and Rothmans and Cathay Pacific in the game, things had changed forever.

Both Jock and Ian were outspoken characters who appreciated rugby but they were in this for business promotion. It was their money and they would make sure they had their say.

There were many fractious meetings and frayed tempers. Tokkie was a strong character with an extremely stubborn streak. He could get a bit stroppy, especially after a few drinks. An open bar and generous refreshment, of course, went with the meetings. "Stubborn bugger," was often muttered. He became very exasperated with Vernon, who was also a super-assured character but who was now becoming accustomed to instant obedience. Vernon was expected to stand back as the policy-making president, but was always coming up with brilliant ideas. He would just turn up. Then he had to take over the meeting and give direction.

While Vernon might drop in and get dictatorial, Tokkie was inclined to storm out raging about resignation. It was left to the hard-working and calm executive members, Secretary Mike Pratt and Treasurer Bob Gaff, to restore the peace. Tokkie's common half-joking discussion-closer was his renowned, "Well, Peace on their heads!"

Once again, Tokkie struggled with the details which were Mike and Bob's forte. Plus, in theory they were doing this in their spare time. This all led to some friction.

Traditionally, the honorary secretary of the Union had kept the files and records, written most of the letters and in practice run the day-to-day show. This was Mike's chore and one which would expand dramatically for successive secretaries in the years ahead. All just for love of the game!

HONG KONG RUGBY FOOTBALL UNION
OFFICE BEARERS 1975/76

President	V O Roberts
Vice Presidents	H M G Forsgate
	P E Hutson
	T A Roberts
	B F Slevin OBE QPM CPM
	D Newbigging
	Sir Douglas Clague CBE MC QPM CPM TD JP
	Lt Gen A.J. Archer OBE
Chairman	A D C Smith
Hon Secretary	M H Pratt
Hon Treasurer	R Gaff F.C.A.

COMMITTEE

T A Tory	representing Club
P Ferry	representing Police
Lt Col T Inman	representing Army
Cdr J Madden	representing Navy
Flt Sgt D Davies	representing RAF
W Trotter	representing YMCA
F D S Humber	representing Valley RFC
A. Reeve	representing Junior Rugby Unio
W R T Lewis	representing H.K.S.R.F.U.R.
D Evans	representing Colony Selectors.

COLONY SELECTORS

D Evans (Chairman)
P Duncan
P Ferry
Flt/Sgt D Davies

Later in the year, time got short and the executive had to make a decision. It was not a question of whether to defy the powers that be, rather that sponsorship funds were available now covering travel and accommodation and must be seized.

How about facilities? Vernon Roberts and Bob Gaff admittedly did bring a lot of weight. They were president and chairman of

The essential details men, Gaff and Pratt.

the Football Club, which owned the clubhouse and stadium. None of this could happen without their full support. Vernon could also freely utilise the resources of the mighty Land Co.

Tokkie had spent decades meeting rugby players from Australia, New Zealand and all over the Pacific and Asia. They were friends listed on his Rolodex and just a phone invitation away.

The pieces all came together.

Tokkie, Bob Gaff and Mike Pratt documented the arrangements and received Vernon Roberts' final blessing.

They then finally briefed the seven impressive senior VPs personally – all close friends who had been in the discussion from the beginning – Gerry Forsgate, Peter Hutson, Tommy Roberts, Brian Slevin, David Newbigging, Dougie Clague and General Arche.

Then he called on the other 10 committee members who represented the clubs and associates, to join them in a formal resolution.

They made that critical decision to go with the Sevens and sent out the invitations!

21

Founding the Sevens

AFTER all the clandestine scheming, the Hong Kong Rugby Football Union came out into the open with a press release in February 1976 calling it the Rothmans Cathay Pacific International Rugby Seven-a-Side Championship, advising that 12 countries had been invited and all had confirmed their participation.

Significantly, neither of their friends Australia nor New Zealand was embarrassed to be invited as a country, but were represented by Wallaroos and Cantabrians, both of whom Tokkie knew well from past Colony games. They ended playing each other for the Sevens Championship anyway.

A large, enthusiastic and very busy team of rugger friends sprang into action to arrange the tournament.

Asked about team accommodation, this time Vernon said, "Put them in the Excelsior!", which was then also owned by the Land Co. The Mandarin was now by far too expensive and posh!

Thus, it lost out to The Hilton on Garden Road as the Sevens gathering point.

A heavy load actually fell upon the ever co-operative Football Club, where the pitch had to be prepared and the Club itself readied for the event. Bob Gaff's problem!

Somehow between them, in just really a few months they pulled it off and welcomed 12 Sevens teams to a one-day competition at the Football Club Stadium on March 28, 1976.

They had come from Australia, Fiji, Indonesia, Japan, Korea, Malaysia, New Zealand, Sri Lanka, Singapore, Thailand and Tonga, with Hong Kong as the home team.

The game programme boldly advertised it as an international championship and listed countries as attending. No wonder the RFU was still fuming years later.

They had their chance and had let Sunshine Rugby slip through their fingers. It had been left to Hong Kong to seize the moment and provide the stage for this joyful and unconventional revision of the game.

However, that was it. The sun did shine and Champagne Rugby had been spectacularly uncorked.

Chairman Tokkie was widely quoted saying it was the most colourful day of sport he had ever seen. It certainly did put Hong Kong on the international sporting map.

It became apparent to them immediately that they had changed international rugby forever. The Scottish Rugby Union Centenary Sevens had hosted all the standard white rugby nations, but the Hong Kong Sevens included nations of all colours, exciting everyone with their high standard of rugby.

It signalled the beginning of the end of white rugby domination and heralded in a new exciting era.

Meanwhile, back at Twickenham, more change towards creeping professionalism. Tobacco had its day and the RFU first sponsorship deal with the Imperial Tobacco had also gone ahead. The RFU club competition, became the John Player Cup at the end of the 1975-76 season.

CREATING THE HONG KONG SEVENS

The Sevens!

Rothmans were delighted they had beaten them to it with the Hong Kong Sevens sponsorship.

Tokkie's statement about putting Hong Kong on the map turned out to be an understatement, and the Sevens flourished and took on a life of its own as the '70s progressed.

Somewhat ironically, in 1977 the colony received a visit by the Scottish national team freshly alerted to the colony as a rugby venue by the Hong Kong Sevens publicity and to explore rugby in Asia.

Tokkie's old pals from Wellington in New Zealand and the Fiji Army also came and the Club had time to tour Australia. So Tokkie was extremely busy.

> **It became apparent that they had changed international rugby forever.**

Rugby was going through great changes internationally and Hong Kong was still at odds with RFU. The Hong Kong rugger crowd had invented their Sevens as they went along and he was worn down by the constant arguments that went into the complicated decisions. It was a stressful and time-consuming volunteer job for everyone!

For example, without enough local consultation, Tokkie had proposed to the sponsors the Rugby Union should invite renowned international referees to the Sevens. The local refs who correctly felt they were doing an excellent job were extremely upset and spoke out angrily.

Tokkie insisted the HKRFU must have the final say on all matters including refereeing, that the referee society was merely part of their organisation and would take instructions from them. Jack Johnston, at the time the referee chairman, spoke out very strongly on behalf of his colleagues and very harsh words were exchanged.

Tokkie attended the referees' board meeting on November 17, 1977 to face an extremely hostile crowd led by Jack Johnston, who also represented them on the Rugby Union board. Jack made an impassioned and angry statement "that the Union had no authority to invite an outsider to referee in the colony and that all refereeing is the right of the society. That any discussion on the subject must be brought to them first and the fact the sponsors had turned the financing down did not detract from the wrongness of the original decision".

Speaking for the Rugby Union, Tokkie praised the referees, said they "did an excellent job and that they should not take notice of the idiots in the stand". Equally adamantly, nevertheless he took the contrary view to Jack and stated that "HKRFU was responsible for running rugby in Hong Kong and the referees were members of the union. They were subordinate to the parent body as indeed they were under the Home Union".

Jack leapt to his feet in anger and totally repudiated this point of view and demanded that they were not subservient to anybody. The minutes report that discussion became extremely heated and personal, raging back and forth. There were demands for apology and pleas to act as reasonable men.

The secretary reports, "Someone, I forget whom, thought it required a certain amount of guts to place one's head on the chopping block as the Chairman of HKRFU did." He concludes that "the meeting broke off more or less amicably".

However, the Sevens were firmly established around the world as a premier, exciting rugby event and the third tournament was coming up. He had devoted five years of his life to the founding, establishing and management of the Sevens, and on the side running the Union. It was taking its toll.

22

Old Friends

SOON after arriving in Hong Kong Tokkie had acquired a British passport and essentially he was to live in Hong Kong for the remaining 24 years of his life. He fully recognised he was living in a British Crown colony.

In practice, the Governor ruled supreme, instructed by his masters in far-away Whitehall and closely advised by a small group of friends who controlled commerce. The rugby elite were well represented. Democracy was a concept practised back there in the United Kingdom.

Even as the British Empire wound down, senior positions in government, the police and business across the globe still went to expatriates. In fact with the loss of territories there was becoming a glut of expatriates and government people needing employment.

They had traditionally been required to play, or at least show an interest in, the gentlemen's amateur game, rugby. The rugby elite in Hong Kong during that era were a quietly well-placed group of very influential people protecting their outdated way of life as the sun set on the Empire.

In those highly privileged days an expatriate would have to do something very public and far out to warrant any police or official attention. They were protected by their status and by being white.

CREATING THE HONG KONG SEVENS

The streets were still rumoured to be controlled by those mystical Five Dragon sergeants, hidden powers in the police force who co-operated with the underworld.

Actually, the recently promoted "Royal" Hong Kong Police Force with the military quietly in the background, was visibly in charge, protecting the colonial system and especially its administrators. Tokkie was personally well acquainted with all their senior officers, and was seen often in the various police clubs.

He was aware of being privileged, but was not too comfortable about how it worked. For example, some of his teammates had left the colony abruptly over the years. Sometimes even inexcusably during a rugger season. It would later turn out that they had been involved in some serious problem, malfeasance or even a potential crime. They had quietly been shipped back home or to another office if valued enough, and the company comprador had reached the necessary financial arrangements with the wronged parties and the local police.

Hong Kong itself was totally materialistic. Business and social life were comfortably non-racist and everyone operated together seven days a week intent upon making a profit; the greater the better. Tokkie knew once you made friendships, racial differences disappeared.

Everyone quietly recognised that the day-to-day life was all just a façade. Below the civilised and controlled colonial surface commerce was raw and cut-throat.

Clandestine deals, kickbacks, payoffs and bribes are the practical Asian way of doing daily business and getting things done. The trusting Tokkie was completely unsuited for that tough world.

The comprador system, agents and partnerships eased the European conscience and helped to prevent the unsavoury reality becoming tiresome cocktail party chatter.

In conducting everyday business and government affairs, everyone

A colonial setting and a privileged elite.

in the general population of Hong Kong was friendly and got on well irrespective of racial background.

Tokkie and Terry had a wide variety of close friends, many Chinese of course, and spent much of their time outside rugby circles being involved in society generally and entertaining for business.

In that colonial setting, the privileged expatriate group he moved in was a tiny percentage of the population but with powers way out of proportion to its size. Their social set held their own exclusive gatherings away from the madding crowd.

Within that little society the rugby crowd had considerable influence and the Smiths found themselves at the pinnacle of that heady company. Their whole way of life, livelihood and self-esteem now depended upon their status in this group.

Their problem was that they were having a struggle keeping up appearances. While Tokkie was pleased to see others doing so well, he constantly struggled with his own comparative business failure.

His rugby vice-presidents, executives and advisors had grown in number and were an impressive group of maturing and close friends, several going back 20 years to the original Gloucester Hotel Bar days.

They were on casual, first-name terms. Close personal and family relationships had formed over the years and they all moved in the same social set. These were very successful people headed by his President Gerry Forsgate, a well known communal and business personality who had been one of the first rugby leaders to whom Vernon had introduced him.

Sir Douglas Clague, known by his friends in those Gloucester Bar days as Dougie, was a war hero and entrepreneur running venerable Hutchinson Whampoa Group which was founded in 1863. Unfortunately he had recently been too entrepreneurial, had taken on serious debt and was in the process of losing his entire corporate empire to local upstart Li Ka-shing.

Brian Slevin, the Commissioner of Police since 1974, was a longtime colleague and rugger man. Although a heavy drinker and generally disliked, he got on fine with Tokkie and supported him through all his years in administration.

David Newbigging, Tokkie's fellow second-row forward at the beginning, was now no less Taipan of Jardines. Approachable and one of the guys in the bar, David was respected as a powerful businessman and crown prince of commerce in the colony.

As Tokkie knew, he was also the tough character you wanted playing beside you in the second row. Long ago, drinking after a game they had heard David's tale of his recent adventure in a Formosa dock bar. It was packed with American sailors, one of whom persistently and inadvisably hectored him about his refined limey accent.

David Newbigging.

Trevor Bedford.

Finally frustrated, the statuesque David felled him with one punch. There was a moment of worrying silence then the bar erupted into applause and back-slapping. David had just moved into the senior level of Colonial administration being appointed a member of the Legislative Council.

Trevor Bedford, his equally aggressive prop, had recently replaced the deceased Vernon Roberts as manager of Hongkong Land. Trevor, one of Tokkie's closest friends, had enjoyed a notable prior career in the government.

Also a character, he had once been kidnapped on government business in the New Territories and dragged off into China. He appeared in the news, bound, with a fierce, ragged and scowling brigand waving a machete over his head. He was very forthright and must have upset the fellow in some way.

Another friend, Denny Johnston, he of the first beer in the Football Club, had been Club captain and Colony selector, was a surveyor and held a senior government position.

Once the calm police fullback, Jack Johnston, was now a braided cap officer. He deserved the braid!

The administration was well aware corruption had become endemic, especially in business and public services such as the police force, and had formed the Independent Commission Against Corruption to fight it in 1974.

It was beginning to have positive results and a police chief superintendent had actually been charged and jailed. However corruption was still out of control everywhere.

Jack Johnston.

The volume of arrests in the Police became so great that in 1977 Governor Murray MacLehose was forced to reach an amnesty with them or risk law and order. In the depth of those unsettled times Assistant Commissioner Johnston had taken on the daunting senior appointment of Director of Criminal Investigation.

Cheerful and happy Tommy Roberts, had been the Club scrum half when Tokkie arrived. He was now the obviously very successful building partner at a leading firm of architects, and was seen managing major development projects. Tom Harley, who had introduced 'Frizzles' Frisby more than a decade before, was now a well-established insurance company chairman.

Dr John Stonham, Tokkie's companion on so many tours and subject of so many stories, had become a renowned medical specialist.

Fellow workhorses for the Union, Denis Evans, Glen Docherty, Bob Gaff and Mike Pratt, were all very successful qualified professionals. General Arche was, well, a general!

There was in addition the large hard-working committee representing all the various clubs and referees that he dealt with daily. Plus the selectors. Then a legion of volunteers and helpers all needing attention.

They were all his daily companions and friends. He loved working with them but it took all his time. It was becoming apparent, even to him, he absolutely must fit in more business.

※ ※ ※

Even his little sister Beth had succeeded in her own enterprises.

She built up a career as Beth Narain, successfully managing the popular Peninsula Hotel disco nightclub. Then she owned fitness establishments and once hit the headlines seen punching friend Bruce Lee on his iron-firm midriff.

Several years after the innocent hand-holding drama at Repulse Bay, she had married her cricketer Moni, this time with the racist

They looked across at the Club.

disapproval coming from his family. They produced two beautiful little girls.

Tokkie had become friendly with Moni and actually had given Beth away at their wedding. He did apologise to her but they were estranged, rarely met and were never really friends again.

Still, the expatriate parties just went on and on. There was plenty of booze and the rugby crowd socialised together and enjoyed those establishing and exciting first years as the Sevens gained momentum under Tokkie's chairmanship.

In March 1978, Tokkie was finally relaxing. First, he would take the Hong Hong team to Tokyo for the All Japan Sevens tournament and then would host the Third Hong Kong Sevens just a month away in April. They were all dressed up to attend the wedding of Denny and Lena's vivacious daughter Leslie at St John's Cathedral.

The extravagant and joyful wedding bash was a short walk away and it took over the Hong Kong Club. Of course the entire rugby crowd was there and in full party mood.

They had all now reached senior management level and the Club fairly buzzed with elevated egos and self-confidence.

CREATING THE HONG KONG SEVENS

Tokkie willed the rain to stop.

Roberts died soon after the 1977 presentation to Fiji.

Tokkie had to admit he enjoyed being a celebrity. He and Terry moved around the gathering telling rugby tales and confidently enjoying all those friendships built up through so many years together. This turned out to be Tokkie's last major social event as the leader of rugby in the colony, and appropriately hosted by his constant friend Denny Johnston.

The day ended at the prestigious Jockey Club, with a large absolutely riotous dinner at a racetrack window table, looking across Happy Valley at the Football Club stadium, the scene of so many of their triumphs. They were all superbly happy and he was on top of his world!

A month later, Governor MacLehose proudly proclaimed the third Sevens the largest sporting event of its kind in the world, which you might expect him to say, but that was backed up by the *Guinness Book of Records* which recorded it as the largest international rugby tournament.

It was indeed growing. Tokkie was proud that four additional teams had been invited from Papua New Guinea, Western Samoa, Hawaii and far away Bahrain. They all added to the exotic flavour of the games.

It had become a weekend festival of rugby and the voluntary workload for everyone had become too stressful.

Tokkie gave a very public appearance, revelling in his position as chairman. At one point kitted out in his Colony blazer and tie, he jogged out onto the waterlogged pitch, getting soaked through and receiving a big ovation for willing the pouring rain to stop. It did not.

The presentation of the now internationally coveted Hong Kong Sevens Cup to the muddy and soaked Fijians and the festive evening that followed was the highlight of his career and of his life.

His years as chairman had exhausted him. He had not realised until Vernon Roberts had died the previous year, how much he had depended upon his mentor for friendship, support and it now appeared, protection.

The new President Gerry Forsgate was an old friend but things had been far from smooth between them.

With the third tournament another great success but before his annual term in office had ended, Tokkie finally did resign and storm out. This time he did not return. His place was taken over for the remaining months by a previous chairman.

By now the Hong Kong rugby business had become formalised.

No longer were decisions just made at the bar nor was there a struggle to raise a quorum for meetings. With the status and financial significance of the Sevens, the board had grown dramatically in size and election had become a publicly recognised honour.

More, it was an assured invitation to 'The Box' for the games and a prominent seat at 'The Dinners', to joke nonchalantly and be seen with the important people.

Tokkie was stepping back from the Hong Kong scene but after his long career he was leaving the international rugby world a very different place.

This was not now the same old historic, staid, white, public school rugby played in the cold. This was now the game of change, of optimism, of self-confidence and of emerging free nations, played in the sun.

It was dynamic. Players' race or culture was irrelevant; their positive mental attitude and pure joy in the game were infectious and proving a winning combination.

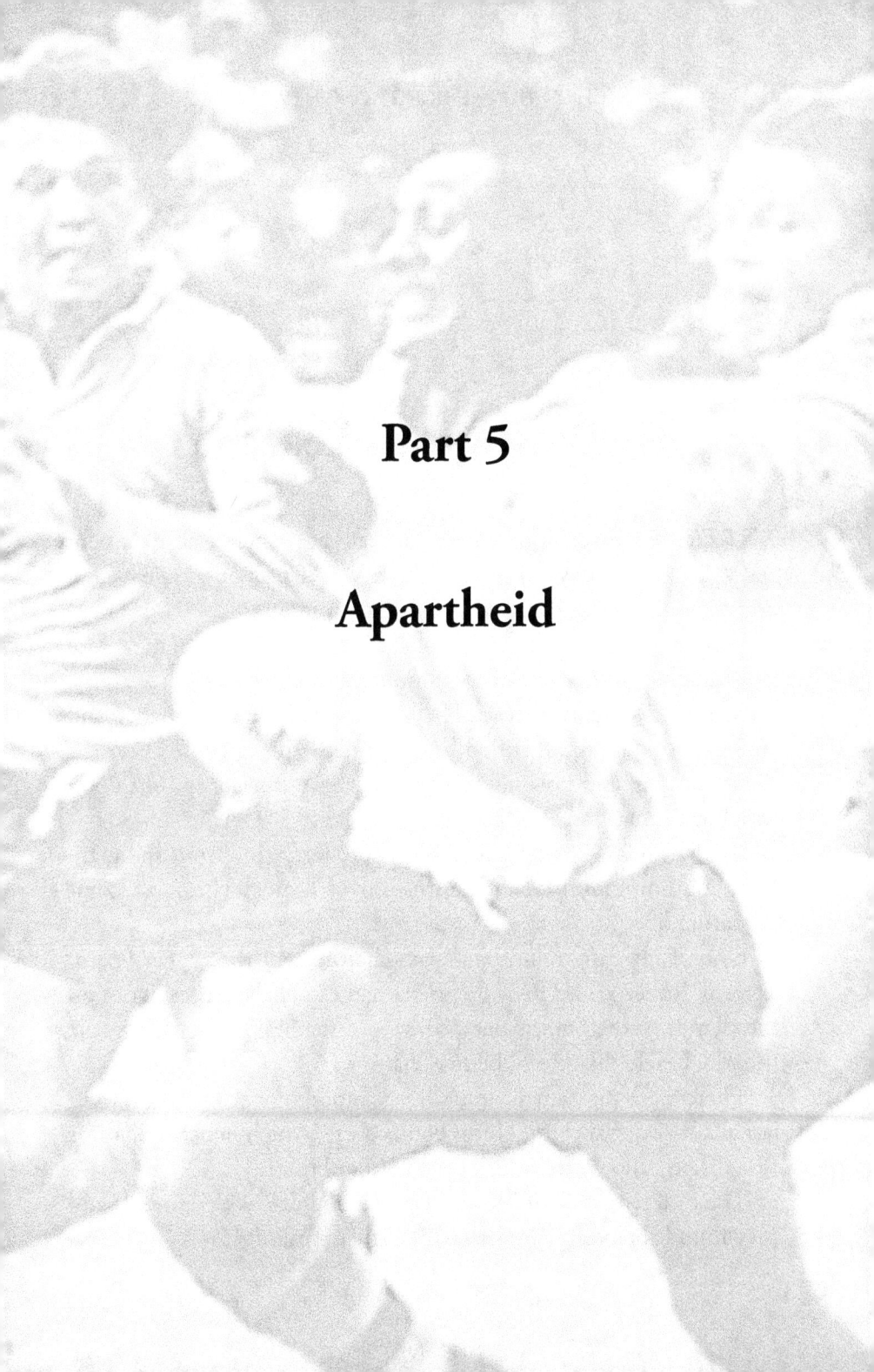

Part 5

Apartheid

CREATING THE HONG KONG SEVENS

23

Prestigious Years

WAY before the impressive bridge, all that concrete development or the massive airport, Lantau was a pleasant, quiet, rural island, home to rice farmers, fishermen and monks.

Long, long ago Tokkie had joined his first team and tramped the two hours up to the top of the mountain to the Po Lin monastery, for a male weekend retreat. They endured the hard benches and constant loud gongs, fortified by the endless spring-cooled beer the silent, smiling and bowing monks must have carried up, but upon which they made an absolute killing.

By the mid-1970s Lantau was a short ferry ride from the main island but important for the Smiths provided much cheaper accommodation.

One of his first friends and past chairman of the rugger board, Tommy Roberts, and his wife Sheila had established a residence on the island, so the Smiths decided to join them. They settled in the friendly beach village of Cheung Sha.

There were pleasant little nodes of modern apartments and villas, all an easy walk from Tong Fook's store, which housed Charlie's Restaurant, known to locals as the Lantau Hilton.

The different style of life attracted several of Tokkie's friends and they found themselves in very convivial community.

Tommy Roberts with Vernon.

With those stressful Sevens years behind them, Terry looked forward to living a 'normal', calmer life with Tokkie home more and friends just dropping over for dinner. They were members of the Police Mess on the island where there were regular lunches and parties at weekends.

Tokkie was known by his fellow islanders on Lantau as, "that rugby-mad South African". They all dined in Charlie's Restaurant, smiled down on by curvaceous current film star heartthrob Virginia McKenna, whom Charlie claimed visited and raved about him and his cuisine.

The restaurant did have excellent food, but the main attraction, brought out later on a Saturday evening was Charlie's collection of vintage ports. Where they came from and how long they had been there no one knew except that the older, dustier and dirtier the bottle, the higher the asking price. Tokkie was renowned as a shrewd port negotiator.

There was a bad hillside fire which threatened their settlement

The playful Stonhams.

and was quickly moving closer. Everyone ran out into the garden for safety but Terry shouted in alarm that their beloved dog was still in the building. Brave Tokkie ran back in and later emerged with his arms full of his rugby trophies. Terry was furious but the dog survived and the story became a part of the Tokkie rugby legend.

Irresolvable bitter differences with other board members had caused him to resign suddenly as chairman in 1978. He was not to take a part in Union activities again until late in 1980. He was however still a member of the Asian Rugby Football Union council and attended all local rugby occasions and games. He was generally referred to in the press as Mr Rugby, and assumed an elite rugby status but it would be fair to say he had essentially been frozen out of rugby administration. However, he was always the centre of attention, surrounded at the bar, and brimming with rugby stories.

On a South-East Asian tour two doctors came along: Stewart Rance for rugger and John Stonham, now a prominent rugby board member, for 'personal medicine'.

The noisy, heavy-drinking group had the back of the plane and the 'personal' doctor stood up to announce he would confidentially dispense precautionary pills on request 'just in case', but they would not be needed by the married and well behaved.

He actually gave out dye pills that made everyone who privately took them pee bright orange. A secret no more.

After the tour Dr John was accosted by an irate woman at a cocktail party who claimed loudly that his 'silly vitamin pills' had stained and ruined all her husband's underwear. She might have added two sets of rugby shorts as well!

One morning, after a national Japan against Hong Kong game, Colony manager Tokkie woke up very hungover and remorseful. The party had got more than usually out of hand and he vaguely remembered Shiggy Konno the now-dignified Japanese chairman down to his shorts performing *Singing in the Rain.* He saw Shiggy at breakfast. He bowed tentatively to Konno-san. "Great party," beamed his host.

Tokkie was himself looked upon as an older statesman in the bar, modestly boasting to newcomers about attracting leading national teams from outside Asia in 'his' years, beginning so long ago with the All Blacks' visit in 1963, and more recently with England in 1971, Wales in 1975, Scotland in 1977 and then France in 1978.

Those were happier days when his frantic years as Chairman were behind him, his much smaller business was under his personal control and he and Terry could take some time for travel together.

So what if he drank rather a lot and was showing it with a bit of weight and a puffy face? Life was good except for the persistent lack of cash.

Things had lost their excitement and perhaps for that reason he was getting bored and drinking even more heavily. His playing days were long over, he was smoking and not exercising enough. His once-regular squash games were now few and far between.

His relationship with Terry appeared to friends to be mutually affectionate but they were embarrassed to witness occasional heated upsets and arguments. They liked to party hard and he could get difficult and somewhat belligerent when he had a couple too many.

The two things that gave him self-respect and held his life together were his fond relationship with his lovely Terry and the high regard in which he was held by his rugger peers.

He was in the process of destroying both.

24

A Return to Africa

SOON after leaving the chairman position and with so much more time on his hands, in 1979 he visited South Africa with Terry. This was his first trip back in 17 years and he was looking for business.

Since he had been away, the disturbing apartheid situation which he had rejected had not really improved, even in rugby. He had expected great change and this was more shocking when he compared it to the open game he now took for granted.

It was quickly apparent to him that he was a celebrity in this rugby-crazed South Africa but more importantly this brought him big commercial business opportunities.

He knew that during the time he had been away South Africa had progressively placed itself in RFU's bad books due not only to apartheid but also to suspected creeping professionalism.

As Tokkie had experienced, the game was getting more competitive and more robust. RFU would say more brutal. They blamed this to some extent on a loss of the gentlemen's game ethic and a determination to win at all costs.

This they decided was leading towards a professional sport which they deplored and they kept finding evidence of payments to coaches,

CREATING THE HONG KONG SEVENS

The Commonwealth Heads of Government and below their agreement.

The Gleneagles Agreement on Sporting Contacts with South Africa, 1977

The Commonwealth Statement on Apartheid in Sport, better known as the Gleneagles Agreement, was issued by Heads of Government from the Retreat held at Gleneagles in Scotland during their London meeting in June 1977.

The member countries of the Commonwealth, embracing peoples of diverse races, colours, languages and faiths, have long recognised racial prejudice and discrimination as a dangerous sickness and an unmitigated evil and are pledged to use all their efforts to foster human dignity everywhere. At their London Meeting, Heads of Government reaffirmed that apartheid in sport, as in other fields, is an abomination and runs directly counter to the Declaration of Commonwealth Principles which they made at Singapore on 22 January 1971.

They were conscious that sport is an important means of developing and fostering understanding between the people, and especially between the young people, of all countries. But, they were also aware that, quite apart from other factors, sporting contacts between their nationals and the nationals of countries practising apartheid in sport tend to encourage the belief (however unwarranted) that they are prepared to condone this abhorrent policy or are less than totally committed to the Principles embodied in their Singapore Declaration. Regretting past misunderstandings and difficulties and recognising that these were partly the result of inadequate intergovernmental consultations, they agreed that they would seek to remedy this situation in the context of the increased level of understanding now achieved.

They reaffirmed their full support for the international campaign against apartheid and welcomed the efforts of the United Nations to reach universally accepted approaches to the question of sporting contacts within the framework of that campaign.

administrators and, even worse, to players. South Africa was one of their top suspects.

For their own reasons the RFU put up with this and never moved to expel SARB from the International Rugby Board. They seemed totally at a loss to know just how to act with respect to apartheid.

There were many Tests and international tours planned in those years, but increasingly arrangements were cancelled due to exclusion of coloured players.

Like all the rugby world Tokkie had followed these dramas and the news of cancelled tours and controversy in South Africa surrounding apartheid and the resulting effects on the game.

By the middle of the 1970s sporting visits to South Africa had slowed such that rugby pals told him the republic desperately needed tours. These discouragements were working but in no way yet appeased the United Nations or the Commonwealth.

Britain had 'lost' another 14 countries during the 1970s, several notable rugby-playing nations. That left just an handful of territories and attention was turning to the newly prominent Commonwealth.

The British Commonwealth of Nations was already starting to gain momentum around the time Tokkie first arrived in Hong Kong in 1959. Most of the nations that had gained independence from the United Kingdom had progressively joined and it had emerged as a powerful political and trading power.

South Africa had been a member, but on account of apartheid its membership had been allowed to lapse in 1961. There was considerable reluctance to re-admit the country or have anything to do with it.

The Commonwealth had opened its administrative office in London in 1965 and it had developed a significant influence in international political affairs. It was particularly incensed by apartheid.

In their Gleneagles Agreement of 1977, the Commonwealth Heads of Government used very plain language to outlaw racial prejudice and discrimination in sport and to foster human dignity everywhere.

They stated clearly that apartheid in sport was an anathema and while acknowledging each country's sovereignty suggested avoidance of any sporting activity with South Africa.

By these late '70s Tokkie was pleased to see that games between teams of different colours were tolerated and becoming more frequent in South Africa. In addition to the all-white SARFB there were now three other rugby unions representing black and coloured players.

Changes were happening and around the time Tokkie's Sevens had started, Danie Craven had softened his stance and selected the first multi-racial South African Invitation team. This had contained four non-white players and beat a French side in Cape Town.

The breakthrough would be a black Springbok player!

With the scene changing so much, Tokkie started to visit South Africa more often on his own, seeking business. He met many old friends and saw some good signs of integration in rugby, but recognised too how difficult it was to achieve rugby change in an abnormal society.

He was soon in the heady company of the leaders of South African Rugby. This led to a personal chat with the great Doc Craven and Tokkie's whole perspective on life changed. For Danie, he was a gift from heaven.

They had faced extreme political pressures, being denied tours in all the major rugby countries since 1974. Now the Gleneagles Agreement discouraged teams from coming to South Africa at all.

Tokkie revered Danie, to him the biggest name in rugby. Dr Craven's career in the game – as a player, coach, long-term chairman of the country's rugby and former chair of the IRFB – was legendary.

By sheer force of personality and persuasion he had kept the precarious Springboks a member of IRFB and on the international scene. South Africa still had Tests, national games and tours, and that might be where Tokkie could help.

Dr Craven had just turned 70 and was impressive and awe inspiring to Tokkie. So when the Doc chatted him up about the need for those touring teams and added nonchalantly that money was no problem and that he could easily arrange generous South African sponsors, the cash-strapped Tokkie listened with growing interest.

Danie Craven

In rugby, Tokkie found he was a popular international celebrity, with his increasing rugby friends all over South Africa buying the drinks, hanging onto his every word and applauding his adventures, especially about the Sevens to which they could not be invited.

In business, he was presented with several opportunities, particularly a new proposal to export food products from South Africa. He threw himself energetically into starting those endeavours.

In love, he had met the most gorgeous young psychologist in Cape Town with whom he was now passionately in love and having a wild affair. This added to his incentive to take more frequent and longer trips to South Africa, while leaving unsuspecting Terry safely far away on Lantau.

25

A Good Try

IT HAD been drummed into Tokkie as a kid that rugby had been the salvation of white South Africa when it drew the English and Dutch together in a common sport after the Boer War. It gave the Afrikaners an opportunity to kick the daylights out of the snooty English guys but make it up in the bar afterwards.

Rugby could help make this happen again, he thought, and unite the present country. All it needed was a few more beers together.

Apartheid upset him and was a negative factor each time he returned. Strict sanctions on trade had been threatened but not yet imposed on South Africa, so he was reasonably comfortable his business operations were not subject to direct challenge. Just a bit dicey!

If racial harmony could best be encouraged in South Africa through integrated sport what better than to bring a demonstration team right into the Afrikaner heartland? He had all the contacts; he could do it.

He was finding his business was growing mainly through his South African rugby contacts and the closer he could get to them the better chance he had of doing bigger deals. It was obvious there was money in this.

He had not been in Asian business for nothing and of course knew that he was being played by the charismatic Danie Craven. He also recognised that he missed being in charge of a rugby activity and was itching for a new sports adventure.

He had been a senior and respected member of the council of the Asian Rugby Football Union for six years and on November 17, 1979 he formally proposed to them that Asian Rugby send a team to South Africa.

He pointed out that Asian Rugby would present the excellent example to South Africa of being the only Union founded on truly international lines, now being composed of nine nations each of different races, religions and outlooks. However, his proposal was "not too enthusiastically received", he reported back to South Africa and it was turned down.

To be clear, the committee expressed concerns about political implications and recorded politely, "That although the suggestion was laudable and that the ARFU stood for the fostering and promotion of rugby football, the time was not opportune to undertake such a tour".

He was not going to give up and by that December he was in serious correspondence with Alex Kellermann, the secretary of South Africa Rugby Board, and Dr Craven regarding another possibility that a multi-racial South African team attend the Asian rugby tournament in November 1980, and tour Asia, although neither Shiggy nor the Hong Kong Union was yet aware of these exchanges.

Alex agreed the South African team would obviously be composed of players of all races, possibly from South Africa Country, Gazelles, Junior Springboks, and Barbarians as selected by the South African Rugby

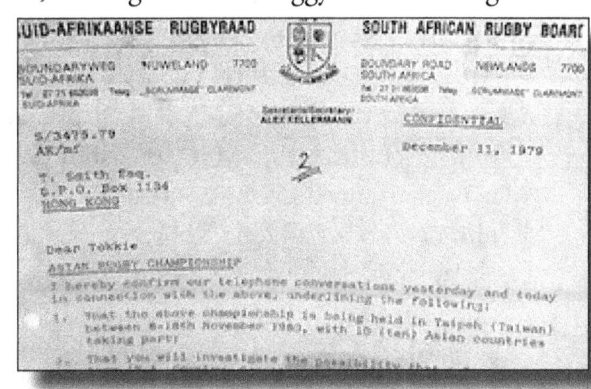

A private correspondence.

Board. The SA Barbarians had recently returned from an extremely successful October UK tour which they undertook with eight each of black, coloured and white players, as it happened so diverse that few spoke English as their primary language.

He suggested a similarly colourful South Africa team could be invited to play a combined Asian team after the tournament. It would be a wonderful exhibition of unprejudiced , open rugby. Tokkie added enthusiastically they should also arrange prior games in Korea, Thailand, Hong Kong, Taiwan and Sri Lanka all of whom he was sure would be receptive to the idea.

In March he made a serious pitch along these lines in writing to Shiggy who found the idea "too premature" and quickly rejected it.

He was getting rather desperate for support and started lobbying widely. He commented to South Africa that various Asian committee members were just discussing the idea with him to give him face but with no intention of taking action.

At that time he accepted a controversial invitation to join a formal tour of South Africa with the World Team, a selection of individual players arranged by the South Africans. This action would soon have him deposed as a Hong Kong representative on the Asian RFU.

By now, back in Hong Kong the Chairman Denis Evans was getting very concerned and contacted Asian Rugby and members directly to clarify that Tokkie was speaking as an individual and definitely not for Hong Kong Rugby. He called a meeting to discuss the situation excluding Tokkie even though technically he should have attended.

Then, came an unexpected bold newspaper headline, 'Hongkong and Asian tour by Springboks', over a well-informed story by writer Austin Daniel. He reported that Hong Kong and other East Asian countries were likely to be visited by a South African representative side later in the year.

Naturally, it was suspected that the false story had been leaked by Tokkie although he wrote to vehemently deny it and state that "his loyalties were first to Hong Kong rugby and then to Asia, not to any other countries".

Denis however wrote a very clear letter to Shiggy Konno in which he reiterated the Asian council's decision there would be "no tour either to or from South Africa involving an Asian team in the immediate future". He clarified that the new initiatives Tokkie saw fit to press were without any authority.

A brilliant opportunity for open rugby is lost

He pointed out the political complications of the Asian nations becoming involved with South Africa and feared such action would be disruptive to the unity of the organisation. Their political alliance was finely balanced.

He asked Shiggy to make it very clear to all Asian nations that Hong Kong was absolutely opposed to any rugby tours involving South Africa.

Tokkie's referee nemesis Jack Johnston followed Denis as Hong Kong RFU Chairman that 1980 summer. An agitated Tokkie wrote him a long letter in July, with voluminous backup documentation, saying that it was all a misunderstanding and had caused him both distress and anger. He was aware his reputation among his rugby peers had slipped very badly, and he was terribly disappointed they did not understand him or embrace this opportunity to further integrate world rugby.

However, in the new season came a very pleasant call. Jack

Johnston, showing no animosity, generously invited Tokkie to manage the Hong Kong team at the Asian games to be held in Taipei in November 1980. Around the bar, much of the sentiment supported Tokkie who was looked upon as a players' representative rather than as a member of the rugby establishment.

Journalist Austen Daniel rushed to report 'Tokkie Smith to manage rugby team in Taiwan', complete with photographs and an expansive piece about his service to the game and applauding that "One of rugby's old faithfuls is back in favour".

But quietly Tokkie was still scheming. This was a critical turning point in his life and he was determined to open up the game.

Should he defy the Gleneagles Agreement and take on the mighty Commonwealth? Like all life's decisions, it was undoubtedly a combination of many things. The clincher was that he desperately wanted to get back to Cape Town for more action with his alluring lady friend.

He made his decision and started secretly to assemble a high-level 'rebel' international team and planning directly with South African colleagues for a series of games in apartheid South Africa.

26

Secret Plans

THE affable and courteous Gerry Forsgate, super successful in business, continued as President. Tokkie had got to know him well since the long ago Gloucester Hotel Bar days and once had counted him as a close friend. Now they had their differences and were distant. Gerry was to be president for a remarkable 24 years.

Tokkie's Sevens founding colleague Ian Gow had lasted just four years as a sponsor. Rothmans, only ever in it for the publicity and the tobacco sales, had reviewed their policy and withdrawn, again from far away in London.

This provided a wonderful opportunity for the Hongkong Bank which joined Cathay Pacific Airline as sponsor, making it an all-Hong Kong and significantly an all local rugby establishment affair.

The Union's day-to-day management also had moved into other keen younger hands such as Malcolm Coates-White as Honorary Secretary. But Tokkie and his old friends were still most of the powerful and respected vice-presidents. By now, these had grown to a dozen with the prestige of the Sevens.

President Forsgate.

Tokkie never had a good relationship with ex-Welsh international Denis Evans who followed him in 1978 as Chairman for two seasons. He was generally very popular and had risen to prominence in the colony coaching the team against England in 1971.

No doubt it rankled with Tokkie that Denis disputed the oft-repeated story that the Sevens had been dreamed up by Smith and Gow over a drink at the Hong Kong Club, rather than by Denis and others at a regular prior rugger luncheon. This was just one irritant but they clearly did not get along. Now Denis was a Vice President.

Denis Evans.

They had been joined by prominent banker and rugby enthusiast Willie Purves, General John Chapple and Peter Wight from the Club. Peter Duncan still headed the selectors.

Roy Henry had taken over the position of Commissioner of Police and had replaced Tokkie's long friend Brian Slevin, which was later to prove significant.

Jack Johnston had been back in the news in connection with his new popular and competent police boss, Roy Henry.

The police had gone through tumultuous times generally but the terrible 1970s were behind them. Among Jack's first and many duties as Director of Criminal Investigation, had been to set up a Special Investigation Unit SIU, which had been ordered to take action against homosexual activity in the colony.

Demonstrating the chaos they were still in, SIU then managed to badly botch their enquiries and also somewhat inadvertently let slip they were also investigating many top people including the Chief Justice and Commissioner Henry himself.

This was exciting considerable press interest but Jack had sensibly extricated himself long before and was off administering the Kowloon area.

This was a new board and the scene was being set for a rugby drama that would personally involve each of them and ruin Tokkie's life. Secure for the moment, his Past Chairman status still put Tokkie on the head table. He could enjoy a more relaxing time taking part when asked, but it was not quite the same as running things.

He saw himself as a leader, but his intransigence and increasing ill-temper had taken the edge off several of his close friendships. Daily stress was wearing him down and relationships were suffering.

He was particularly upset that he was falling out with Trevor and Shirley Bedford who had been his closest friends for 20 years. Trevor had replaced Vernon Roberts at Hongkong Land which was in the Jardine family.

David Newbigging himself was at the top of Jardine which Tokkie considered had raided his original company and taken away all his key clients. Both David and Trevor were now over-assured and successful businessman.

In addition they were all vice presidents in the rugger scene but where Tokkie, as recent Chairman and the Sevens founder assumed a superior status.

All of these issues were leading to a very uncomfortable relationship between these old friends.

Not knowing the nefarious things Tokkie was up to while away on his trips to South Africa, unsuspecting Terry was still living happily on Lantau.

This was where, late in 1981, Tokkie first confided in Colony and Sevens star Chris Wynne-Potts and revealed his ambitious secret plans. Chris was a young police inspector and had been recently posted to

Chris Wynne-Potts in uniform and in action.

the island. He lived near the Smiths and often dropped in for a beer or a meal on their balcony.

Tokkie insisted this was all to be highly confidential but he was planning a mixed-race 'rebel tour' to South Africa. It must be kept quiet because there would be a backlash due to the politics regarding apartheid, which might prevent it from happening.

He asked Chris to join as an individual not representing a country, as all the players would, in the planned first multi-racial international rugby side ever to tour South Africa.

Just recently Tokkie had been very angry when, at the request of Government House, a Cape Town schoolboys rugby touring team had been forced to cut short its visit to Hong Kong by the Union.

This was reported to be on account of the colony's apartheid policy, so he was aware it was a sensitive subject.

Also the Springboks' tour of New Zealand that year had ended in chaos when anti-apartheid demonstrations had caused two games to be cancelled and police to use force to control crowds.

These events did not deter Tokkie. He explained it had been agreed in South Africa that he was to be organiser and manager. The plan had been arranged with Danie Craven and various other rugby stalwarts from that country and was formally supported by their rugby union which was affiliated with the IRFB.

Admittedly South Africa had just received an enormous setback, following that New Zealand tour, when IRFB had banned the Springboks from any international tournaments until apartheid was abolished. But this was just a tour.

While general trade sanctions were not yet imposed, there were many political and business inferences to be drawn from the tour, especially as Tokkie, using his Sevens experience, would finance travel and expenses through sponsorships.

That the tour was paid for by apartheid-supporting South African business would have deterred lesser mortals, but not the stubborn Tokkie!

Once again the concept looked great; the details would work themselves out.

Danie was on record recently warning his South African colleagues, "We are now closing a book and entering a new era, South Africa will never be the same again. You know we must make changes towards a multi-racial deal not to placate or pander to overseas opinion but because it is the right thing to do."

Tokkie believed that his friend Danie Craven had indeed changed his colours, at least regarding rugby.

Several influential South African businesses were offering to act as sponsors including a shipping line owned by Jardine of Hong Kong.

Tokkie realised this might be an embarrassment for his rugby friends who were Jardine directors.

He had also been told the South African Government offered special tax breaks to sports sponsors that covered a lot of the cost. It was beginning to be difficult to keep this a purely rugby matter.

However, he had been careful to arrange financial support that was common on rugby tours, where players and officials were remunerated only for travel costs and supplied with accommodation and meals, plus playing kit and uniforms, such as blazers, ties and shirts.

They would travel strictly as amateurs and there would be no payments for the players. The coach, assistant staff and security would be provided and remunerated in South Africa by Dr Craven and Tokkie would be 'well taken care of' as organiser.

He managed to keep all this planning highly confidential. Players would be asked only to request three weeks' vacation and must never mention South Africa.

It was clear to them any sporting contacts with that country at least conflicted with the spirit of the Commonwealth Gleneagles Agreement. But surely the mere act of introducing a mixed-colour team to play rugby in South Africa far outweighed those silly politics?

He convinced Chris Wynne-Potts, who agreed to go but was worried that there could be many problems around the whole apartheid question. That easy decision in the sun, over a few beers, would dramatically change his life.

Now all Tokkie needed was a team!

27

The Brilliant Islanders

In 1977 Tonga grasp the Plate.

TOKKIE'S experience as a player had been a progressive education within the rapidly evolving rugby world around him. While he was an administrator he would play a pivotal part in changing that world.

From unnaturally cloistered rugby as a youngster in segregated South Africa he had moved to a more liberal team make-up in England. Then he went on to enjoy the open attitude in New Zealand and Australia. Now he had spent half a lifetime experiencing the rich cultural mix of Asian rugby.

CREATING THE HONG KONG SEVENS

The Asian RFU, which Tokkie had a part in founding in the 1960s, did not include the Pacific Islands such as Fiji, Western Samoa and Tonga. They had been playing rugby since the 1920s, some much earlier, but were isolated and mainly within the influence of New Zealand.

Their location was remote and historically had been difficult to access. In Hong Kong, a Fiji Army side posted to the colony played in the Blarney Stone Sevens games in the 1950s, before Tokkie's time. He had not been exposed to playing with the Islanders. However, their unpredictable, fast style of play was well known.

It was an outstanding decision to invite them to the Hong Kong Sevens and both Fiji and Tonga accepted.

At that time, Sevens was a small, developing part of the game. That first International Sevens he had been so upset to have missed, had been held at Murrayfield only the year before and was still an all-white game.

While the mini-game had been catching on in Europe, neither New Zealand nor Fiji for example, were to have serious national Sevens competitions until after the Hong Kong Sevens started.

Shiggy Konno said Japan was not into Sevens and wondered why they had been invited.

So why did Tokkie's committee include Fiji and Tonga? It was not their Sevens reputation because they were not particularly into Sevens. Yet! They were indeed nations, if recent, which helped with the international sponsorship conditions Rothmans demanded.

The fortunate timing of all these events was quite amazing. Just recently in 1970 Fiji had not only celebrated its independence with a triumphal UK tour, but Tokkie was aware they had beaten the Barbarians. Indeed, they must be good.

In April 1971, celebrating RFU's centennial and recognising spreading international inclusion, old pal Typhoon Sir Ramsay had selected two Fijians in his international President's Overseas XV which

Western Samoa rush.

Fiji won 1977 Cup.

convincingly beat England at Twickenham.

More recently back home Fiji's national team had excelled against the touring England side in 1973 and the All Blacks in 1974.

That had encouraged Tonga, just the year before the Sevens was dreamed up, to tour the UK, demonstrating Tonga's exciting game to a wider world and playing against Welsh and Scottish representative teams. Tonga had become a nation in June 1970.

The European tours had reminded Tokkie and his board of the excitement and flamboyance the Islanders could bring to the game.

The effect of those invitations upon the Hong Kong Sevens and the rugby world was to be staggering!

They certainly were fast learners! In the opening Hong Kong games Tonga made it to the Plate final, but Fiji were knocked out in the semi-final of the Cup. They went home and worked on national Sevens tournaments. The following year in 1977 Tonga won the Plate and Fiji won the Cup!

They were joined by other Island teams, notably Western Samoa, as the tournament progressed year by year. They all performed brilliantly. Tokkie formed many close friendships with them during those early Sevens years and they were now important to his plan.

28

Finding the Dragons

IT WAS essential to Tokkie that the nucleus of his team must be composed of non-white players. He had the business plan in place with his South African friends, so he set out in the autumn of 1981 to find players.

For a tour the following year he found his selection options severely restricted. Obviously he could not extensively approach Asian rugby players without causing more trouble. He thought of Maoris but Australia would be touring New Zealand then and he could not get anyone to commit. Similarly, Fiji would have a Test series in Australia. He particularly needed Pacific Islanders, so he concocted a reason for a trading business trip to Tonga and the other islands. He was already friendly from the Sevens with the Tongan coach and chairman, who also happened to be conducting import/export business with him.

Over drinks after a game, the coach asked Tonga's star player, Alamoni Liava'a – who was Tokkie's prime target – if he and two companions would like to go on a tour in South Africa? Co-incidentally the coach was also Liava'a's 'Boss'.

The young Tongans were ecstatic and the commitments were made that evening. Could they get time off? Of course, their Boss said!

They were concerned about visas on account of their colour and their new nation status but Tokkie said he had been assured all

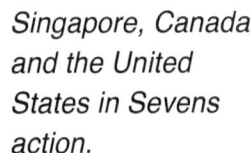

Singapore, Canada and the United States in Sevens action.

necessary travel documents would be supplied by the South African Government.

The arrangement was to be in total confidence but no sooner was he off the island than everyone knew.

Next, in nearby Western Samoa, Tokkie desperately wanted the fastest man in the Sevens, Taufusi Salesa, and was jubilant when he and another support player signed up.

Now he had not only the essential mixture of players he needed but also, he thought cheerfully, the calibre of players that could beat South African provincial teams and make the country take notice.

He confirmed to Danie Craven that the tour was on for July 1982.

Tokkie seriously wanted an Asian included and he knew it was ironic he had to reach outside Hong Kong for a Chinese player. The most prominent Chinese undoubtedly was the captain of the Singapore team, Song Koon Poh, but Tokkie did not get a chance to talk to him until the Sevens at the end of March.

The Singapore national team had played in the first Hong Kong Sevens and KP skippered the all-Asian team in 1979. They had performed very well and once making it into the Cup quarterfinals.

Rugger had been adopted by the Singapore Government as a rugged sport to build character and was included in the school curriculum. Local kids like Koon Poh benefitted from training programmes devised by the Rugby Union, which produced a strong national side by the early 1970s.

With experience, Singapore had emerged as a respected rugby nation in 1978, spectacularly beating the Hong Kong team of expatriates with an all-Asian team in the final of the sixth Asian Cup held in Kuala Lumpur. This firmly established rugby as a national sport and Koon Poh as a star.

KP was again captaining the Singapore team at the 1982 Sevens tournament when his friend Tokkie approached him with the invitation to join the South African tour.

Being a young Asian lad he was spellbound by the invitation but said he would need a few weeks to think about it. How in the world could an Asian be invited to play in apartheid-controlled South Africa, he wondered?

Tokkie told him the invitations were so secret he could not divulge the names of the team but assured him they were high-calibre players. This was intriguing and a great adventure, so he joined.

Filling out the team, Tokkie also discussed the subject generally with David Batemen of the American Eagles national team, which had made their debut in the 1981 Sevens. He would get back to Tokkie.

How about the Canadians? Initially in the first few years of the Sevens, Canada was not included. Their appearance was in the 1980 tournament where they went out by a respectable 10 points to Australia in the quarter-finals.

Tokkie was no longer chairman by then, but he became firm friends with several of the Canadians and particularly with Ro Hindson and his family who were from South Africa.

Canada was a stalwart of the Commonwealth and a supporter of the Gleneagles Agreement. Ro told Tokkie Canadians felt that politicians should keep their hands off rugby.

Back in Canada, Ro was farming away busily in the beautiful Okanagan Valley and received a telephone call from Tokkie that the tour was on and he readily agreed that he would take part.

Hans de Goede, the Canadian hooker, signed too. Their renowned winger Spence McTavish joined them when they called for backline reinforcements.

They all played for Canada and provided Tokkie with the status of an international-quality team. For their part, they were confident they were setting off on an honourable venture.

He still needed another world-class prop and he heard that

Australian trialist Sandy Muston might be available. Sandy received a telephone call from him in Sydney and, disappointed at not making it on to a Wallabies tour, he immediately agreed to go. At the South African Embassy Tokkie had everything arranged. Sandy was treated as a celebrity, received priority visa treatment, his passport was stamped and he was on his way. Plus he made the neat arrangement with Tokkie that his wife and young son would join him in South Africa at the end of the tour.

David Bateman came through with a large contingent of Americans and Tokkie had his team.

Actually, he had the players but to turn them into an effective team he needed leadership. He had been very impressed with Mike Luke the captain of the Canadian national team when he came to Hong Kong to manage the Canadian squad at the 1981 Sevens.

When Mike readily agreed to come on the tour to skipper and lead the Dragons he knew he had his winning combination.

Dave Bateman

Tokkie confirmed they would be a mixed-race team but only he knew who had been invited. They were to assemble in Johannesburg in July 1982 for a three-week visit and would be pitted against powerful provincial sides. There would be no pre-publicity and all planning was totally secret.

It would offer a tour of that magnificent country, a chance to meet its varied people, and particularly an opportunity to make a practical demonstration of mixed rugby in the country.

All expenses would be fully paid by sponsors. Who could resist!

29

A Secret Arrival

THEY slipped quietly into the country at Jan Smuts Airport in Johannesburg.

Tokkie, enjoying the limelight at the airport, issued a statement to the press, "There were no rugby unions or rugby boards involved, although we do expect to be entertained at some time by officials of the South African Rugby Board. The players are here as individuals that love the game and just want to play rugby."

A South African paper, improving the story, reported it was sponsored by two anonymous South African businessmen. This made things worse, adding intrigue. Each game was to be well advertised and promoted by local posters, which quickly became collector's items.

For Tokkie this was a wonderful moment in his rugby life. He had brought an international team to play at top level in his home country.

It was especially exciting for the team members who had no idea who was in the team other than their own countrymen, until they arrived. Many of the players were old friends from international competitions and it was a boisterous welcome.

But it could have all ended right then!

Beaming, and flushed with excitement Tokkie hosted the welcoming drinks and dinner party. He became so excited that in trying to eat, drink, and shout a welcome at the same time, he choked on his

Singapore's Song Koon Poh meets Danie Craven at SARB welcome party. In the background is Mike Sherlock of the USA.

Springbok Dave Stewart (left), who coached Tokkie's Dragons, with Song Koon Poh, ex-South African captain Morne du Plessis and Kouliti Ma'u from Tonga.

steak and fell gasping to the table. It was actually a serious situation. He could not breathe and started convulsing.

He was extremely lucky someone there knew the Heimlich Manoeuvre which had been around for only a few years. Even more, that the strong American player David Bateman could perform it successfully on such a burly person. It threw a complete damper on the evening and the tour got off to muted social start. Tokkie made light of it but he felt the effects for days.

Before they left Johannesburg they were all treated to seats at the final game of another rebel tour. An unofficial group of rugby stars from the Five Nations tournament in Europe had accepted Danie's invitation to play in South Africa and finished their tour with a game against a selected Springboks team.

South Africa was celebrating the opening of the new impressive Ellis Park Stadium and had invited the presidents and officials of England, Scotland, Ireland, Wales and France Rugby Unions who had no compunction in accepting the lavish trip.

The celebrities were royally entertained and had been received in Pretoria by the South African Government on July 23 to discuss legislative changes to make conducting sports in South Africa more inclusive. Now they knew all the fuss about Gleneagles Agreement had to be nonsense!

They flew together as a team for Cape Town to get serious.

Mike Luke, a very responsible person, found himself in daily charge of a spirited, independent group of young fellows determined to succeed but have a great time doing it. For the entire tour he felt he was herding cats.

Immediately upon landing they knew this was no ordinary tour. This was a military police state and although they had been invited by the sound rugby lobby there were volatile right-wing extremists strongly opposed to things like liberal rugby and adamantly

Dragons waiting for the bus to training in Cape Town. From left are Paul Grey (Western Samoa), Peseti Mafu (Tonga), Singapore's Song Koon Poh, Hans de Goede (Canada), Canada's Spence McTavish (obscured), and Sandy Muston (Australia). In front is Taufusi Salesa (Western Samoa).

against mixed-race cohabitation.

Some members of the tour were actually frightened by the atmosphere and were initially reluctant to even leave the sanctuary of their hotel. No one knew yet what reaction there might be at the games when a mixed-race touring side appeared.

First multi-racial South Africa rugby tour

As a gesture, Mike went to a township rugger club for a training session and found it disconcerting to be surrounded totally by masses of black people.

Everyone was friendly, the visit went well and the discussion was all about the game.

He encouraged the team to stay totally away from politics and concentrate on discussing the tour. They all believed they were proving that rugby could be a great unifying force.

At Newlands stadium in Cape Town. From left: Alamoni Liava'a (Tonga), Song Koon Poh (Singapore), Peseti Mafu (Tonga), Chris Wynne-Potts (HK), Paul Grey (Western Samoa) and Mike Luke (Canada). Up front is Kouliti Ma'u (Tonga).

They were housed at Newlands, were measured up for their kits and outfits and were welcomed personally by Doc Craven. They would immediately start hard training for their first game, under provided coach Dave Stewart, a South African national centre, and star Springbok captain Morne du Plessis.

Everything was arranged, meticulously planned and paid for by the South Africans. The sponsors themselves benefited from the generous government tax arrangements, which clearly demonstrated the political nature of the venture. The administration was managed by a very serious gent named George, complete with office and calculator.

The players were not remunerated but received $10 per day from George as pocket money, then a sufficient sum.

Art Ward from USA.

CREATING THE HONG KONG SEVENS

Tokkie was delighted when George produced team jerseys with a distinct dragon emblem on the chest. Tokkie's Dragons! He was upset when it was pointed out to him it was not in fact a Dragon but rather a heraldic Lion Rampant, which was the company logo of their cigarette sponsor. Everything was sponsored!

George was not only the 'go-to person' for everything but the holder of the purse strings. It became a continuing, cheerful battle with him for the players to have expenses approved. He got into a particular fight with the Americans who had nonchalant spending habits anyway and ran up thousand-dollar phone bills.

George beat them down but the Canadians on the team disliked the Americans' attitude and considered them obnoxious. This is of course a common opinion of their neighbours to the south.

The Americans who came along were Dave Bateman, Mark Deaton, Art Ward, Gary Lambert and powerful prop Mike Sherlock.

The four Canadians were captain Mike Luke, Ro Hindson, Hans de Goede and "Spike" McTavish. Totally different personalities came with the flamboyant Islanders, Kouliti Ma'u, Peseti Ma'afu and Alamoni Liava'a from Tonga; and Taufusi Salesa and Paul Grey from Western Samoa. Tokkie was disappointed at not attracting anyone from Fiji.

Sandy Muston was the Aussie prop from Sydney, Chris Wynne-Potts from Hong Kong, Song Koon Poh from Singapore, and they were proud to include South Africans Tim Cox and Japie Julies, who cheerfully described himself as Cape coloured. They spent the whole trip successfully taking Japie into colour-restricted bars.

Tokkie had assembled a mixed bag of highly talented international players but Mike Luke and Dave Stewart had the job of moulding them into a team in a few days.

30

'A Worthwhile Exercise'

When news of Tokkie's Dragons' tour reached Hong Kong there was an immediate negative reaction and he was telegraphed by the Union to cancel the trip immediately.

This was really none of their business, he thought. It was a private arrangement and carefully in no way linked to them. Anyway, he had no intention of stopping and set out to achieve his objective of breaking down colour barriers but winning games of course.

Socially, the whole event was highly emotionally charged and everyone on the tour recognised it was the racist regime that was being challenged.

They were to play five very strong provincial select sides, starting at Cape Town with Boland and Western Province, then Natal

Tokkie's Dragons.

in Durban, Orange Free State in Bloemfontein and finally Northern Transvaal in Pretoria.

They encouragingly but narrowly won their first game against Boland in Wellington on July 28 but a few days later lost the second game against Western Province 20-7, in a tough slog that saw American international Gary Lambert, who had previously played against the Springboks, carried off with a broken kneecap. He completed the tour hopping around with his leg in a cast but hugely partying and enjoying himself.

Otherwise the tour was going well. Tokkie was proving a serious manager who was all business, although he was not beyond a nip of whiskey for breakfast. His rumoured girlfriend did not make an appearance.

Most of his discipline problems came from the over-assured North Americans who were out in South Africa's notorious bars at every opportunity. Of course, the non-white players could not officially join them, even if inclined. No one commented too much on the irony of the situation considering the objectives of the tour.

As it turned out the Islanders were moderate bar goers. Koon Poh was designated by the Government as coloured and would not risk embarrassing himself.

The white guys often got lucky having access to the bars and returned to the hotel with the women they had met. This provided great entertainment because all the players shared rooms, particularly as one had to perform with a leg in a big cast. Some of the ladies even became enthusiastic supporters, knew everyone and followed the team.

KP took apartheid with reasonable humour which he accepted as possible because he had to experienced it for only a few weeks. He was actually bemused by the whole situation. At home, he was a celebrity known and greeted with respect wherever he went.

Here he was diminished as a coloured, which meant for example he could not use the toilets for whites or blacks, but had to hunt for the less available ones designated for his group. If he was in an hurry he either had to make it back to the hotel or find a quiet spot!

The Islanders were a cheery bunch and made friends with anyone. They found most people, of any designation, to be friendly in return and willing to get around the often-regretted government rules.

They laughed at the observation they were brownish, foreign and different, which allowed the rules to be bent and gave them access to some of the more important bars and nightclubs.

They all dealt with apartheid in their own way, and were united in their mission. They had quickly made friends and enjoyed the banter and comradeship of a successful team.

When Tokkie awoke, that quiet sunny morning in his old home town of Durban, he was excited and anticipated an incredible day of rugby with his Dragons taking on a powerful Natal provincial team, which boasted the current Springbok captain Wynand Claassen.

On another side of the world, in Hong Kong, the high drama had already been played out.

Called to order by President Gerry Forsgate the full board of Hong Kong RFU had indeed sat in silence wondering what to do about their colleague Tokkie. Their own policy on tours to South Africa had been plainly stated and they certainly knew where the governor stood.

Out of their silence came the obvious answer: they had no choice. They voted unanimously to remove Tokkie as a vice-president and cut him totally from Hong Kong rugby, which they well knew to be his whole life.

They announced their verdict by a brief press release which they no doubt thought would end the matter.

The decision reached Tokkie in South Africa as the Dragons were preparing for the Natal kick-off. The published statement read, "In view of this vice-president's unwillingness to conform to the policies of the HKRFU in respect to sporting links with South Africa, he has not been re-appointed as vice-president."

This was followed by another drama when he heard that Mike Luke had to deal with the indignity of their non-white players being refused entry to the team changing room at the stadium for the game.

He tried to concentrate on the game which turned out to be the most exciting of the tour with the Dragons running off, somewhat bruised, but with a 23-22 win. So much for refusing our guys changing space!

It should have been the highlight but now he started worrying about a reckoning. Chris Wynne-Potts was not mentioned and Tokkie thought it did not sound too bad if he was only being stripped of his ceremonial vice-presidency.

At this point the pressure got to Song Koon Poh. Back home in Singapore all hell had broken loose and he realised he was in serious trouble being on the tour.

Prime Minister Lee Kuan Yew was taking a personal interest in the situation being a signatory of the Gleneagles Agreement for Singapore. Mr Lee was not a person with whom to tangle in autocratic Singapore.

Furthermore, KP had been Singapore's Sportsman of the Year in 1978; he was a celebrity and his action was too public to ignore. His employer, the multi-national Shell, had also been brought into the discussion and he valued his job.

He became international news when Reuters reported chairman of the Singapore Rugby Union, Howard Cashin, had stated, "I feel very strongly about this matter and I told the committee we should not hesitate to take strong action against Song because of his status. He has kicked us in the teeth and we will look silly if we do not act firmly".

KP's wife also worked for Shell and called to warn him this had become a very serious public matter back in Singapore. He stayed for the important Durban game but then caught the next plane home.

Dragons captain Mike Luke runs into trouble against Natal. In the background is Spence McTavish.

Too late.

※ ※ ※

The Dragons went on to win the fourth game in Bloemfontein at the prestigious Orange Free State Stadium as an opener for a Currie Cup match. History was made when the provincial select team against them fielded two black players for the first time ever. It was claimed in fact, that it was the first time a black player had even set foot on the field. Tokkie was delighted and for him this progress alone made the entire tour worthwhile!

Finally, on August 11 they lost to Northern Transvaal in Pretoria but still with the consolation of winning the majority of their games.

There were social events after each game and a large beer party was given for everyone involved at the end of the tour, all celebrating together, making their last emotional farewells and vowing to meet up again one day. This included serious George, their long-suffering and harassed administrator, finally letting down his hair and being uncharacteristically cheerful, possibly because it was all over!

Orange Free State selected first black players

They recognised and toasted the victory they were achieving over apartheid.

※ ※ ※

Danie Craven was renowned for his personal charm. Showing his very human side, on learning Mike Luke was an academic, he invited him personally to Stellenbosch University.

He devoted the day to discussion, much of it in his famed study and presented Mike with a copy of his much publicised physical education doctoral thesis.

※ ※ ※

A very serious uniformed detachment of Special Branch Police, white of course, had been assigned to travel with them and watch over things. They became friends and personally attached to the players. At the end of the tour they brought their families to the airport to see them off, hugging the very popular Tongans and Samoans.

The team received a goodbye telegram from the South African Rugby Football Board: "Tokkie Smith and members of the Dragons team. We thank you for touring South Africa. All members and their national teams are welcome to tour this country at any time. May you have a safe journey home. Regards, SARFB."

Somewhat dismissive of the problems the tour would undoubtedly cause them, Danie Craven telegrammed on their departure: "Tokkie. It was a worthwhile exercise. The members of your team were an advertisement for rugby and their countries. Bon voyage. Come again. Craven."

Always a very emotional person, Tokkie had tears of joy rolling down his face at the airport, as had happened often on the tour. He flew back to Hong Kong with Chris, happily convinced he had made a strong statement for integration in South African rugby.

CREATING THE HONG KONG SEVENS

Part 6

Judgement

31

The Reckoning

ARRIVING back in Hong Kong, Tokkie and Chris Wynne-Potts found they were in big trouble.

The President had stated that Tokkie had been removed by unanimous decision from any further connection with the Union. He followed up with an explanatory statement that they had no choice and were bound by the Gleneagles Agreement, the International Olympic Committee and the Commonwealth Games Federation.

They could not quite bring themselves to publicly fire him: "He has not been reappointed as a Vice-President", was the sugar-coated way they put it. Conveniently the AGM had been in May and they could really just not include him in the list of VPs to be appointed.

He just could not believe it: unanimous? On something like this everyone had to be consulted. The weight of the decision would have been on the 18 officers who were all long-time colleagues. He knew each of them well and counted them as friends.

But he particularly could not understand the twelve Vice-Presidents who were his close personal pals from his decades in local rugby. They had totally abandoned him without even talking about it. Friends of a lifetime!

He should not have been surprised. This was not only about rugby. With an elite as close as this, you have to decide if you are

in or out. Tokkie was out.

He could hardly have chosen a worse time to launch his provocation! The last thing chairman Jack Johnston or especially his VP and police boss, Commissioner Roy Henry needed now was more controversy. They certainly did not expect this to come from rugby. To add to the overall police miseries the SIU botched investigation had tragically resulted in the suicide of a young gay Scottish police officer early in 1980.

The whole affair was highly publicised in the colony but also in the raw London press and came to the highly critical notice of their master, the Foreign and Commonwealth Office, FCO.

The resulting MacLennan Inquiry was the most expensive in the Colony's history and ran to mid-1981. It put the police force and the Commissioner through the wringer. Everything had been satisfactorily contained and hushed up but Governor MacLehose and particularly FCO had been far from amused.

Within a year of this major upset, Tokkie had chosen to

defy the still-sensitive Administration and the Commonwealth Office by setting out on his South African adventure. To add to his problem, a brand new Governor, Sir Edward Youde, had taken office that very summer, just when the police-led Union Board was called upon to decide Tokkie's fate. As might be expected they were all falling over themselves to act decisively and to impress Sir Edward.

Not that the new Governor was yet paying any attention to this minor matter. He was preparing his Prime Minister Margaret Thatcher for her historic meeting concerning the future of Hong Kong, to take place the following month in China with Deng Xiaoping. Things in general were getting tense.

Tokkie felt devastated, without friends, and ever emotional. It broke his heart. But he was not totally alone.

By very good luck his closest, longest buddy of all Denny Johnston, although a skipper and Colony selector had not been directly involved. Therefore he was spared the indignity of having to make that decision and with several buddies stood by Tokkie.

Denny was a dour Scot from the tradition of George Heriot's School in Edinburgh. He had no time for BS and tended to be somewhat anti-establishment. If anyone would come to Tokkie's support at a bad time it would be Denny.

Tokkie was even more upset and guilty to hear that in Singapore the keen young Song Koon Poh had suffered a similar fate being found to have "committed an indiscretion and breach of discipline as captain of the national team".

KP had been banned from rugby or coaching for life, also without a hearing and while he was in South Africa. How many young lives had Tokkie ruined?

Singapore was absolutely not a place where you could defy authority and win. KP wisely kept quiet, settled for an abject apology and stoically took up the marathon. He was quietly encouraged that he was not stripped of his Sportsman of the Year title, although that was debated. A lot was written, with an eye to local politics, citing his arrogance in having toured South Africa while ignoring his duty to the country as team skipper. A few brave souls understood and supported him, notably, to his great relief, his employer Shell, which saw no reason to take any action.

The Pacific Islanders were questioned back home for having gone on the tour, but argued successfully they were opening up the game in South Africa to coloured players. In any event, the islands had some important games coming up and needed their leading players!

Tokkie and Chris faced a media storm with newspapers initially critical and supporting the actions of the Rugby Union. They both appeared on television to defend their positions, but faced only criticism.

This was all exacerbated by Tokkie's high profile with the Sevens which was now an enormous success and had just relocated with great publicity to the larger Government Stadium at Sookunpoo.

The Hong Kong press, still following the story closely, jumped on the unexpected resignation of the Union's respected Secretary Malcolm Coates-White, suggesting ominously this was, "before the dust has settled on the South African affair".

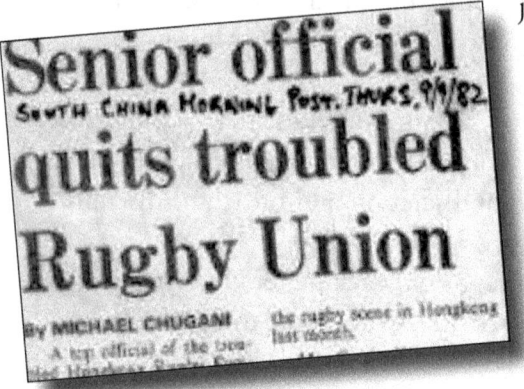

In his honorary position he actually organised the Sevens and was the spokesman for the Union in a stressful, time-consuming job. Tactfully he merely commented, "I need a break. I just want to be out of it!", and left.

In fact his leaving had nothing directly to do with the Tokkie affair but was rather the result of boardroom infighting which caused his resignation and resulted in the appointment of Denis Evans and Associates to start administering the Sevens professionally in October. The Union was run from the top, was then very dysfunctional, and it did not help that two assertive board members represented the Sevens sponsoring companies.

Chris was potentially in very serious trouble and was being formally investigated on a possible criminal corruption offence for accepting accommodation on the tour. Sensibly he had bought his own air tickets.

Jack Johnston, as a senior police officer, had been put into

an impossible personal position as Chairman of the Union. The Government and police had an official policy in this matter and he had his orders. Further, Chris had defied the mighty Mil-Pol and had the temerity to ignore their 'suggestion' he quit the tour.

The police had its own powerful internal rugby clique which fortunately prevailed. Chris was issued a reprimand and their rugger side happily retained him on the team. After all, with the season starting he was a needed star player. He was also a shoo-in for a repeat place a few months later on the Hong Kong Sevens team which he had represented in the three previous tournaments.

Later, came the shock. The Union was not as forgiving as the police team and would not be selecting him in the Sevens team for 1983 apparently on account of the South Africa tour. This caused a storm of speculation in the media.

Tokkie was incensed and reacted angrily in the press and TV interviews. "Gross cowardice on part of the Union," he thundered. "Absolutely the most appalling and disgraceful decision. Just what is going on?" His attitude did not endear him to the establishment!

Gerry Forsgate replied with a terse public statement that Chris Wynne-Potts had been excluded as a player again by unanimous decision because of "risks inherent". That was all they had to say and proved not very clever because it increased speculation.

Tokkie blasted back, "I believe the public has the right to know why our best player has been banned and Hong Kong is fielding a team which is not our strongest. Pressure must be applied and this cannot be allowed to be swept under the carpet."

Press discussion revolved heatedly around the possibility of government and big business influence because the Sevens had just moved to the larger Government Stadium and of a sponsor threatening withdrawal. They all naturally denied any interference and insisted this was solely a Union matter.

The sponsors did opt for clarity and added, "The sponsors were appraised of the problem by the HKRFU. We made it clear to the Union it was a matter for them." They then confused things by jointly stating to the press they did not wish to be embroiled in an international political dispute.

The reporters pointed out to Peter Duncan, the Colony Sevens coach and selector, but who was not on the Board, that four countries would compete against him and contain players who had gone on the tour. Chris Wynne-Potts had announced he had been invited informally to play and was in training. All a perplexed Peter could do was to shrug and say he had to abide by the policy decisions given to him.

The Union had advised all the Sevens countries about the Hong Kong situation and suspensions. All of this was reported as far away as the *Wellington Post* which commented that other than Singapore where Song Koon Poh was still banned for life, other teams were taking no serious action. Even the Soon Koon Poh dismissal passed its board only by a 10-5 vote and only then when chairman Howard Cashin bowed to the establishment and threatened to resign.

Chris Wynne-Potts was a big, strong and tough fellow as one would expect of their best player. He was still in his mid-20s and had been thrown into a conflict going all the way up to Government House. "This is sheer hypocrisy," he complained to *The Post*. "I just want to play rugby."

* * *

The American Dragons players seem to have coasted through all the political rugby fuss unscathed. America was not particularly concerned what the British Commonwealth thought. They were in the middle of a worrying recession and in any case they had colour differences of their own to explain.

Dealing with the situation all on his own in Australia, Sandy Muston received no adverse comment about the tour from either his government or the rugby union.

There was short-lived interest in the media, but it mainly developed around the financial aspects of the game and professionalism.

On air, an unsporting radio personality dropped a sensational accusation on him that he had been paid a quarter of a million dollars to make the trip.

Sandy was especially upset as he had received the set $10-a-day expenses to undertake what he considered to be a very good cause.

He took legal action, causing the radio station to retract and settle quickly. Otherwise, he could assure Tokkie he had suffered no personal problems and considered it a very successful trip.

* * *

The Canadian establishment was concerned what the Commonwealth thought, but even in the face of insistent pressure from their Government sponsor Canadian Rugby found it prudent to withdraw life suspensions it summarily imposed on the four invited Canadians.

In the Canadian way, the players put up a rigorous legal defence that successfully claimed that the South African tour offended neither the spirit nor letter of the Gleneagles Agreement and that the ban also contravened the Canadian Bill of Rights.

This all led the British Colombia Rugby Union formally to support their players and they adopted a public position regarding their personal right to play in South Africa. This was accompanied by a two-page reasoned review of the many connections with that country and a denouncement of the hypocrisy being displayed on this subject.

They concluded they did not agree with Federal Government policy. "Canadian industry, and professional sporting interests maintain thriving relationships with South Africa yet we in an amateur sport are dictated to as if the activities of rugby, badminton, and gymnastics have far greater impact and importance then do business agreements involving gold, diamonds, wine and tourism; a rather questionable logic. We believe communication is more desirable than ostracism."

Hong Kong hypocritically fields no Asian players

They were not living in a colony! They accepted a warning and went on playing. They had pointed out that the Canadian winger, Spence McTavish, was the only white player in the Dragons backline!

The HKRFU was seen as hypocritical having no Chinese players and still fielding only white expatriates. In their colonial superiority cocoon they perceived no irony in all this. Indeed they did not select a Chinese player for the Hong Kong side until a decade later.

There were a few moments of relief from all this heated debate with Erika Roe's televised joyous, halftime jaunt without the benefit of her blouse on the pitch back at Twickenham. This was another example of disregard for authority and the demand for new freedom sweeping the world. Tokkie was delighted to hear she was 'out of Africa', just like him.

Further it was announced that women's rugby was being officially incorporated in the UK, dramatically opening up the game. Never the philosopher, Tokkie just grinned and joined in the fun.

Perhaps they were not as stuffy and such slaves to authority and tradition back in England as they appeared? He would get a surprising answer to that question the following year.

■ ■ ■

Tokkie and Chris were each formally persona non grata at the 1983 Sevens a few months later. They bought tickets and very publicly put on a good face, cheering on their friends from the stand, joining in the excitement and drinking too much beer like normal mortals.

They watched with divided loyalty as the Hong Kong Seven was defeated in the semi-finals of the Plate by the Canadian team fielding Ro and Spence from the Dragons. Others appeared for the Eagles and for Tonga and then Taufusi made it to the Cup semi-final and played a brilliant open game for Western Samoa.

Privately Tokkie and Chris knew their days in Hong Kong were numbered. Chris was finished in the police and was returning to Africa. He was offered a job in Johannesburg, he resigned and left a few weeks later.

Now clearly rejected by their establishment friends, Tokkie and Terry also accepted that their life in Hong Kong was over and started planning their own move to South Africa.

32

Alone

IN TOKKIE'S defence, it can be pointed out that the South Africa ban was not absolute. Danie Craven managed to keep South Africa in the International Rugby Football Board throughout the entire apartheid era. The Dragons had been welcomed and recognised by the legitimate South Africa Rugby Board which the IRFB itself could not find the fortitude to expel.

Notwithstanding the Gleneagles Agreement in 1977, there was the British Lions tour in 1980 continuing a tradition started in 1891, then France, followed by Ireland in 1981. So Tokkie's Dragons had not been alone.

In organising the tour he had gone to great lengths not to involve or alert anyone in local rugby specifically so the Union would not be implicated. All the players were attending as individuals and were not representing any club. They were all on vacation.

In their wildest imagination no formal association could be charged with sending a representative team called Tokkie's Dragons.

They all knew Tokkie was far from racist and that years before as skipper he had gone out on a limb to combat the feisty, imperialist President Colonel Dowbiggin to get Bill Leong into the Club. The farcical interplay of Tokkie and the Colonel, such entirely different characters, had provoked mirth in the bar for years.

For more than two decades Tokkie played on and helped promote tours and had formed close friendships with players of many races.

He was very proud that he had set up the gloriously non-racist Sevens. The year he took his group to South Africa the Hong Kong Sevens had welcomed teams from the UK, Canada, Scotland, USA, Australia, Fiji, Tonga, Western Samoa, Indonesia, Korea, Muscat, Malaysia, Hong Kong, Japan and Thailand.

Incorrectly, he thought his record would speak for itself, but he had been totally rejected. He did not fully appreciate that the success of the Sevens had propelled him into the limelight and that he was now an international celebrity. His name was so closely associated with Hong Kong rugby that anything he did would reflect back upon the Union.

They had decided they could not hide his transgression or overlook his action. Chris by association with him became collateral damage, although the police saw him as a disciplinary problem.

What hurt Tokkie most was that they had not even given him a chance to explain before acting so publicly.

Then came the final blow to Tokkie's self-esteem and reputation: The List!

The UN Special Committee against Apartheid, was compiling its "Register of Sports Contacts with South Africa", recording any sports people or officials whom they considered despicable for participating in sporting events within that country.

The evidence was gleaned from official records, notices and newspaper reports within South Africa.

The intention was to bring moral pressure on sports activities. It was later seen to have worked, but a listed person or organisation could be taken out of the records if sufficient repentance was demonstrated and there was an undertaking not to return.

The story of The List hit the press in Hong Kong in May 1983 when it was revealed both Tokkie and Chris had been internationally denounced.

Tokkie tried to joke defensively, boasting that he considered it a great honour be in the company of so many famous sports personalities who had defied the ban.

The *South China Morning Post* headline called him a rugby outlaw. It reported that Union outlaw Tokkie Smith had greeted with dry amusement that he was on the United Nations latest anti-apartheid black list. "'I consider it a great honour,' Mr Smith joked. 'It's a very exclusive club but it is getting a bit overcrowded.'"

The report continued that British and American sports figures were prominent on the list, which included entire cricket and rugby teams, cyclists, boxers, footballers, racers, drivers and athletes.

Asked if he would agree never to play again in South Africa and have his name removed from the list he told the *Post*, "No way! Certainly not. It's absolute nonsense." He added that he had no regrets about organising the tour. "There were players from seven countries in that team and they would all go again."

Much of that was bluster and in private he took it very hard. He maintained a brave front but finally that summer, dispirited and totally financially broke, he admitted they had beaten him.

As it happened, some prominent members of his rugby elite were themselves running into trouble as the colony spiralled again into a severe recession. Hubris and reckless optimism had overcome common sense and ruinous financing was being exposed by high interest rates and the sharp drop in demand and value.

The Chinese Government had announced it was taking back Hong Kong on or before July 1, 1997, whatever British Prime Minister Margaret Thatcher demanded. Tokkie decided gloomily he might anyway be better off back in apartheid South Africa.

Fortunes were being vapourised but it was possible for establish-

ment managers to run their companies into enormous problems but still go home personally wealthy. They were isolated from the real, nasty world by employment contracts, retirement provident funds and the reliable goodwill of their well-placed establishment friends.

Colonial officials and government employees were immune personally from financial turmoil as they are worldwide; in Hong Kong with their pensions at age 55 intact, irrespective of the part they may have played in causing the problems.

Not so Tokkie, whose investments were gone, who had no steady income, no assured pension plan to rely on in the future, but worse a ruined reputation.

> **Worse, a ruined reputation.**

He gave up on Hong Kong and with great humility accepted financial assistance from Denny Johnston and his few remaining rugger pals and returned permanently to South Africa.

33

The Morning After

WITH Tokkie and Chris essentially forced out of the Colony, the rugby elite were confronted with the realities of their actions. Did it have to come to this?

To his enduring and close friends Tokkie was a warm, caring person who was passionate about his beliefs, extremely hard working and always a staunch and loyal friend. Others eventually saw him as opinionated, stubborn and totally unreasonable.

Still, even with all the counter claims and jealousy, everyone had to acknowledge he had in practice founded the Sevens and indeed deserved the local title of Mr Rugby. So, how had he managed to turn all his friends so vehemently against him?

When they heard Tokkie's Dragons had kicked off in Boland on July 28, 1982, the Union executive felt he had defied and deceived them. President Gerry Forsgate wasted no time acting. They agreed they were finally all fed up with Tokkie!

A few days later, Gerry called an unusual extraordinary general meeting for August 3, 1982 at Police Headquarters, formally "to discuss the South Africa tour by an Asian/Pacific team managed by a Vice President of the HKRFU".

He told the meeting he had specifically invited all the Vice Presidents. There was a big turnout recorded as T. Bedford, D.

Evans, W. Purves, T. Harley, T. Roberts, G. Docherty, P. Wight and W. Mosley. Consulted but unavoidably absent VPs were R. Henry, J. Chapple, D. Newbigging, J. Johnston (Chairman but out of town) and T. Smith, (apparently not invited!).

Nine directors also attended representing the Police and the various clubs plus Treasurer W. Layfield and Secretary M. Coates-White.

The proceedings were minuted as follows: "The President explained the purpose for calling the EGM and why we had taken the unusual steps to ensure strong representation from the Vice Presidents. The President read the brief from Government on sporting links with South Africa and the Secretary distributed copies to all assembled."

Malcolm Coates-White then described a conversation he had with Tokkie on the topic of a tour to South Africa in which he said Tokkie denied all knowledge of the subject "while being quite vociferous in the process".

Trevor Bedford felt that Tokkie's actions, knowing the HK situation, were reprehensible and the Union should back up its views by strong action. This view was shared by most Vice Presidents.

Tom Harley felt that Tokkie had done a disservice to rugby in HK.

"W. Purves recommended that the HKRFU dissociate itself from the whole affair including Mr. Smith".

The meeting formally recommended that, "a statement be prepared and released to the press advising that Mr Smith would not be re-confirmed as a Vice President. This matter was to be discussed at a General Committee and the statement prepared by the

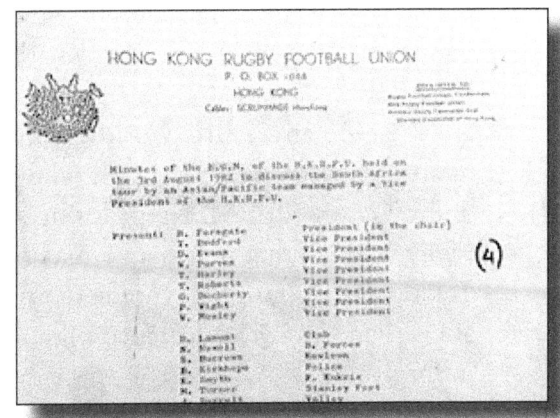

HKRFU Committee once they had deliberated on it, having heard what the Vice Presidents' views were on the matter. The statement would be released in the name of the President and the letter advising Mr Smith of the decision would be signed by the Chairman".

The required committee met immediately following, still at the Police Headquarters, to deal with the details, "confirmed the reappointment of all Vice Presidents except Mr A. D. C. Smith and after much discussion a press statement was prepared and agreed." They then interestingly appointed Denny Johnston as a VP replacing his great pal Tokkie. The press release was issued immediately.

Denny was shocked by the news of Tokkie's firing, but being a confirmed member of the establishment he of course accepted his vice presidential honour.

On September 26 in his *South China Morning Post* editorial page column 'Straight Up', veteran journalist Ted Thomas was forthright enough to suggest why this might all have occurred.

Under the prominent heading, 'Sacrificial Springbok', he wrote, "Rugby players play for fun not money. So how come Tokkie is ostracised? One theory is because Tokkie's brainchild the International Rugby Sevens has become big business. The Hongkong and Shanghai Bank and Cathay Pacific stand to lose millions of dollars in worldwide publicity if any hiccough appears in the arrangements for this increasingly popular event. Remember what happened in New Zealand last year?

"Imagine any Third World country suddenly leading a movement to boycott the Sevens? It would mean big money down the drain. Get my drift? Imagine losing all that money. Tokkie Smith's crime was not that he led an amateur rugby team to South Africa. Tokkie's single-minded crusade to promote international sport has, as everyone knows, threatened big business. That in Hong Kong is unforgivable."

He followed up again a few days later, "Sitting minding my own

TOKKIE SMITH AND THE COLOUR OF RUGBY

business, in my favourite club last Monday sipping a nourishing glass of tonic wine, when I am set upon by a very senior person in the world of rugby with accusations of bias and side-taking in the Tokkie Smith scandal.

"You can bet your donkey that I am biased. Tokkie finds himself with practically the whole of Hong Kong's formidable establishment aligned against him. The other side can take care of themselves and no doubt will. If it's an unbiased opinion you're looking for in this newspaper, read the editorial page."

Tokkie had read about his firing in the press release far away in Durban, but it would be two months before Chairman Jack Johnston had returned to the Colony and reported to the Committee that he had written to Tokkie. He briefly and officially informed him he would not be reappointed as a vice president, ending his outstanding service to rugby in Hong Kong and Asia without comment.

The subject of Chris Wynne-Potts however gave them more personal anguish. Chris was Hong Kong's star Sevens player and universally very popular. Most members of the committee initially expected the problem would just go away. They thought the Union did not concern itself with individual players and that disciplining him would be left to the club involved, as their Secretary had reported at the press conference.

Thus this was up to Police Rugby which immediately reselected Chris and he turned out as usual for their teams. However, more dogmatic and vindictive members pointed out that the Union committee had adopted powers specifically to discipline individuals in October 1978.

The ominously named 'Power 29' was produced and cited, by which the committee could "at its absolute discretion suspend, reprimand, or otherwise discipline any individual player whose conduct infringes the laws of the game or brings the sport into disrepute. No member shall knowingly permit any player under suspension by the Union to play in any of its teams".

The Police RU had decided to take no action against Chris and as the season progressed he was back in their team, actually representing them in the second round of the Blarney Stone Sevens early in 1983 and training for the Sevens.

This time it was not an extraordinary gathering of all the forces but the simple committee without Vice Presidents that resolved, "Due to risk inherent in his selection, as explained to the committee, Chris Wynne-Potts has been disqualified from selection in the 1983 Sevens". Having all been convinced by the mysterious person who explained the "risk inherent" they all importantly but somewhat defensively reported their decision as being carried '*nem con*'.

The press enjoyed a field day! What risk inherent could there be from his selection? Who gave the explanation? Was it the sponsors or perhaps a government edict?

The factions driving the Union had taken things way too far but insisted their decision stood. A defiant Tokkie was one thing. Vindictive action against a star young player just wanting to play the game but caught up in politics was another.

All along they had over-reacted, allowing it to become too personal, political and commercial. Rugby was an amateur sport. By going public they had turned what could have been a privately managed issue into two ruined careers and international news.

34

A Rolling, Bouncing Ball

UNHAPPY and depressed, by August 1983 Tokkie and Terry were in temporary digs in Cape Town. They tried hard to stay together but their financial and personal problems were insurmountable and they separated.

Chris Wynne-Potts had settled successfully in Johannesburg but kept in touch. He was upset when they parted but he was hopeful they might get together again.

However, Tokkie, about to turn 50, still had his hot romantic side relationship going and they moved in together in Cape Town, starting afresh. He was indeed something of a celebrity in the rugger crowd and he began renewing his many South African friendships and expanding his new business.

At this lowest point in his life, when he was struggling to make sense of it all, he just could not believe what came next.

Rejected and depressed Tokkie takes to drink

The RFU was sending the England touring team to South Africa!

England, head of the Commonwealth, instigator of the Gleneagles Agreement and controller of the Crown colony of Hong Kong, was ignoring its own undertaking. How could this be happening?

His tormentor, the United Nations no less, complained bitterly that the United Kingdom was violating UN resolutions regarding apartheid and allowing RFU to wilfully ignore the Commonwealth Gleneagles Agreement.

Back in England, the press and public opinion strongly opposed the tour. There were demonstrations and marches. South Africa intervened politically and 100 Conservative MPs demanded the RFU be allowed to make its own decision. But politicians generally, worried naturally about their seats, sent the Minister of Sport for several meetings with RFU to back down – to no avail.

The United Nations applauded those who attacked the RFU: such as the UN Special Committee against Apartheid, the Organisation of African Unity, the Supreme Council for Sport in Africa, the leader of the Labour Party, the British Trades Union Congress and the British Anti-apartheid Movement.

Finally the big guns. The Commonwealth Secretary General and even the famous Archbishop Trevor Huddleston made their appeals.

CREATING THE HONG KONG SEVENS

The Commonwealth Games Council for England had powers to prevent the tour, but did not act and even appeared to approve.

No one could shake the resolve of the supreme RFU which was still omnipotent in its own mind and voted overwhelmingly to send the national team to South Africa.

So the tourists were also rebels. They arrived in May 1984 but with a team somewhat weakened by the aversion to apartheid, including regrets from their captain Peter Wheeler.

After all those years from Tokkie's youth, Danie Craven had finally yielded – no doubt as a part of the arrangement – and his team was no longer completely made up of white players, which helped RFU justify its decision.

Tokkie was cheering on South Africa from the stands and was absolutely delighted at Springbok wins in both exciting Tests.

He also found himself in good company when the United Nations Register of Sports Contacts declared the RFU tour the most serious violation that year of efforts to prevent apartheid in sport and listed all members of the touring group.

As Tokkie had boasted years earlier to the Hong Kong press he was honoured to be on the list in the company of outstanding athletes. Now it was with the entire England team, but it was a bitter-sweet honour! The English tourists faced no sanctions at home and suffered no penalties. He had lost everything!

Tokkie was not naive enough to believe this was solely a story about rugby, although that was Doc Craven's obsession and main concern. It was not even about the money increasingly being made around the sport. Large international businesses and governments were involved and influencing those decisions from England to Hong Kong to South Africa.

Perhaps there were lingering delusions of an empire lost.

Friends saw things differently here and most of the players of all races Tokkie chatted with in South Africa applauded his Dragons' effort. Still, rugby may be heading the way Danie claimed, but Tokkie had to admit he saw no impression upon the National Party or its oppressive apartheid policies.

With the whole world fighting about these issues, how had he managed all on his own to get himself into this lonely mess? He shook his head and just stared moodily into his beer.

Part of the fun of rugby is trying to judge which way the ball will unexpectedly bounce or roll, but he had no way to anticipate what happened next.

To his utter amazement, just a few months later, the Hong Kong Rugby Football Union had a change of heart. Others were apparently also of two minds. His dark mood was quickly forgotten.

Out of the blue and showing a surprising reversal of sentiment, the Sevens board invited him to return to Hong Kong as a founding hero to celebrate the festival's 10th anniversary in 1985.

Tokkie, Ian Gow, and Jock Campbell were to be feted as founders. Generally, things had finally calmed down in Hong Kong.

The sharp recession had caused business casualties in the elite. Trevor Bedford and David Newbigging, both members of the unanimous board that had so summarily dismissed Tokkie, themselves suffered the same fate and disappeared from the colony.

Thus the times, attitudes and the board itself had changed. Glen Docherty, a long-time and sympathetic friend of Tokkie, had taken over as Chairman.

The board was no doubt influenced by the RFU's South African tour decision the previous year, which conflicted with its own stated policy in Tokkie's case. The pressure was off.

With respect to rugby, Tokkie was down but far from out.

He had publicly switched allegiance and had ambitiously thrown himself into the South African Rugby camp at the top, plotting new moves with his friend 'Doc'. What they had in mind was to expand the Dragons model and for Tokkie to manage a series of international invitation teams composed of top individual players from around the world. He had all the contacts.

He wrote up their ambitious ideas for Danie Craven late in February reporting also that he had received an invitation to the Sevens 10th anniversary in Hong Kong which he happily advised would be at their expense.

He said he had already arranged to meet 10 leading players for discussion on the international individual South African tours at the Sevens on March 30 and 31. "There will be over 250 players and managers from 24 countries taking part in the Sevens" for him to canvass, he added enthusiastically.

He explained somewhat immodestly, "A book is being published on ten years of the Championship and they probably feel that as the Championship was my idea and I ran it for the first three years they can't very well write the book without me, hence the invitation!"

Comfortably now in South African rugby politics he recommended

Forsgate, Smith, Evans, Johnston and Docherty.

as an aside that Doc sought endorsement at IRB of the Hong Kong Sevens as a World Cup rather than support a full team World Cup, which South Africa could not attend and said if he could do anything for him for rugby in London on the way to Hong Kong to let him know.

Tokkie was back in the game!

Delighted to be visiting Hong Kong, Tokkie outfitted himself with a brand new Colony blazer complete with a shining crest, put on his lucky gold rugger cuff links and presented himself proudly again at the Sevens as the smiling, confident Tokkie they all knew.

Five of Tokkie's Dragons had not suffered on account of the tour and were still representing their countries. Ro was there for Canada, David and Gary for the Eagles, and Alamoni and Taufusi from the Islands.

He posed laughing with his three fellow chairmen of the first 10 years of the Sevens, including Jack Johnston who had fired him. They were joined later on the pitch by long-time president Gerry Forsgate, playfully throwing a ball around.

They put on a good face and at least publicly appeared fully reconciled from the Dragons incident. However, they were restrained. Tokkie was caught standing quietly, looking sad, at the back of the official box while the limelight in the front row was shared by his seated, beaming old colleagues Gerry Forsgate, Shiggy Konno, Jock Campbell and Ian Gow.

The Sevens had been established as a wonder of the rugby world, the 10th anniversary matches were brilliant, the after-game festivities were noisy and vibrant.

Trying to overlook the cool reception from the establishment, Tokkie revelled in the toasts and cheers of his fellow players and friends from so many races and countries. Just for that moment, but for the last time, he was back at the top of his world!

CREATING THE HONG KONG SEVENS

A restrained reception and Tokkie relegated to the back row

35

Final Whistle

TOKKIE was renewed, refreshed and ready to take on that world again. He had returned to South Africa, hugged his new love and with a positive attitude started chasing down all his business contacts. He was back!

But his happiness lasted just a few weeks.

His mother also had returned and was living in her home town, Port Elizabeth. On July 12, 1985, he and his lady had been visiting her. After a late dinner and a 'few drinks' they were driving back towards Cape Town on the Garden Route highway.

He dozed off, the car drifted off the road and overturned. He did not survive the crash.

Denny's tearful eulogy.

Tokkie to the end was stubbornly not wearing his seat belt and seemingly not his lucky gold rugger cuff links. His companion was fortunately more prudent and although injured she survived.

His mother and friends arranged a small and modest goodbye gathering and he was cremated in Port Elizabeth.

Even at the end he had missed a couple of details and died intestate and somehow having not quite managed formally to marry Terry. The fact that she came to him with the same Smith surname presumably solved that little problem. His estate was disputed in South Africa with his mother and her children sharing what little was left. After a battle Terry managed to hold on to a flat they owned.

The news of his death quickly spread around the rugby world.

Reporting in the SA *Sunday Times*, writer and friend Mel Channer said, "South Africa lost its greatest East Asian rugby ambassador when Tokkie Smith was killed in a road accident near Port Elizabeth a fortnight ago. Tokkie became a household name in the rugby world circles when he launched the famous Hong Kong Seven a Side Tournament in 1976."

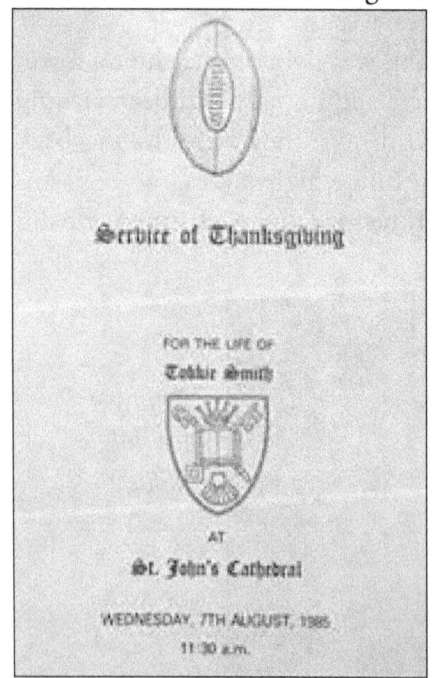

He went on to applaud the Dragons tour in glowing terms.

The largest outpouring of sentiment took place in his adopted home, Hong Kong. It was here his friends of a lifetime lived and where he had achieved the outstanding success of that life, the Sevens.

Those friends, supported by an impressive turnout of rugby players and fans packed his memorial service early in August 1985 at St John's Cathedral on Garden Road. He had never been into religion but it was here, so long ago he had mourned the passing of rugger pals Kim, Bill and Jack.

The following wake naturally was at the Football Club and again was filled *Glowing tributes.* by sad friends and the entire rugby establishment all speaking fondly and nostalgically of his glowing contributions to rugby. Fresh from showering somewhat inebriated praises and adulation upon him at the recent 10th Sevens celebration, they were totally shocked by his seemingly immediate death.

Who else could deliver the eulogy than friend for ever Denny Johnston who tearfully lauded Tokkie's life totally committed to the game.

The readings were by Glen Docherty representing the HKRFU and close friend Jeremy Wilson. There was a thundering organ, the full Hong Kong Welsh male voice choir, and a closing touch which would have delighted Tokkie: a piper playing *Amazing Grace*. The Order of Service sported a rugby ball and the symbol of the Hong Kong Rugby Football Union on the covers. As they later drank to his memory and said their sad farewells the Hong Kong rugby elite were still trying to decide whether Tokkie was a saint or a sinner.

One thing they did not need to debate: He had founded the Sevens, opened up the game and had become a rugby legend!

36

Redemption

TERRY stayed in Cape Town for several years and then moved to the pretty south English town of Farnham, still in close contact and reminiscing with old friends about the happy rugby era they had shared in Hong Kong.

The Old Toffs enjoyed long and happy lives completely devoted to their amateur rugby. 'Frizzles' Frisby saw out his last days celebrated as the RFU's 'oldest living member' and yarning at the centuries-old pre-rugby George and Vulture pub in the City.

Sir William and Lady Nora Ramsay were to be found telling rugger stories in the snug at the Clarendon Inn down the path from their sea-sprayed cottage on The Front at Sandgate.

Danie Craven lived to 82 in Stellenbosch and was the most renowned of them all. He had finally selected black Springboks and like Tokkie he was either a saint or sinner depending to whom you spoke.

He lived just long enough to see apartheid come to a final end.

The Sevens had lost Tokkie, their founder. Hong Kong rugby had also deprived itself of its star Sevens player, Chris Wynne-Potts. Or had it?

After a few years in South Africa Chris returned to work in Hong

Kong. He was playing regularly and thought all was forgiven when in 1989 he was again selected for the Sevens side.

Earlier Chairman Jack Johnston, who had banned him in the first place, was now a VP. Still burdened by his police policy, he reminded his colleagues Chris was subject to a life ban, and after a heated debate they withdrew his selection. It is difficult to sideline your star player on a matter of principle, unless you are senior rugby elite.

Tokkie would have been delighted to know that was not the end of the story for Chris. The next year new officials relented and Chris did represent Hong Kong again in the 1990 tournament. For him, all was finally forgiven!

Chris moved back to South Africa where he lives in sunny Durban. Now, more aware of the inexcusable iniquities of apartheid, despite the good intentions and brotherhood Tokkie's Dragons achieved, in balance he is not sure it was justified. But what a memorable rugger tour!

Song Koon Poh of Singapore too had a happy ending. He had been an extremely popular personality in Singapore and his fall had been sudden and personally devastating.

With a necessary nod from Prime Minister Lee, a couple of years later he had very quietly been allowed back to play and coach again. Shell, which had supported him, benefited by a loyal senior employee for 32 years! After reinstatement, in 1984 he played for Singapore against Canterbury, and at the top of his career in a completely redeeming and crowning performance he starred at home against France.

He remains a renowned sportsman and public figure.

The Pacific Islanders always maintained their moral right to play in South Africa as they again demonstrated in 1987 at the height of international sanctions and increasingly successful sports isolation.

Fiji, Tonga and Western Samoa defiantly formed a combined bank-sponsored Pacific Barbarians team to tour accompanied by guest players such as Ro Hindson from Canada.

They played the SA Barbarians, narrowly losing both games, but they won almost all of their other fixtures. These were against the officially sanctioned mixed-race feeder teams, which did demonstrate that racial change was actually taking place in South African rugby.

Quite apart from the fact that the Islanders themselves were invited to play there!

Peter Duncan, the young coach and selector who was so perplexed by the Tokkie and Chris controversy, later served two terms as Chair and assumed the Presidency of the now-splendid HKRU in 2016. The Union bears no resemblance to the society of those long ago days. Neither, similarly, does the Football Club itself.

In previous times, rugby was essentially a home-away-from-home activity. It was a small-time, all-amateur operation with no employees. It was not uninclusive intentionally but little effort was made to interest local people in 'our' game. Quite honestly, not much interest was shown by the Chinese community either until the Sevens.

That first inclusive Hong Kong Sevens tournament was actually quite a modest event but then achieved international attention through extensive sponsorship promotions. It widely publicised Sevens as a fast, exciting game and it captivated fans everywhere with the skill, agility and pure joy in the game shown by the emerging rugby nations. Naturally, with all the publicity, there was a surge of interest in rugby at home in Hong Kong and the Union eagerly accommodated the demand.

By the mid-1980s many Chinese and other local men were playing the game and they soon started their own teams. Colts, School, and Mini rugby were promoted and women showed they too excelled at the contact sport.

Now, in addition to organising the Hong Kong Sevens annually, and successfully representing Hong Kong, the Union reports more than 80 men – and women – league teams, plus widespread school and minor games involving many thousands of youngsters.

Despite interesting times along the way, the Union has developed into a significant and respected local organisation, involved in an array of public activities and charities. It is a non-profit organisation, channelling all revenue back into the game.

They all rejoice in the vibrant, totally inclusive and multi-ethnic sports community that has been created. For his part Tokkie got no redemption from the United Nations where his name can still be found on The List.

However, in 1995 the then-HKRFU associated in the publication of a beautiful, large glossy book commemorating the 20th anniversary of the incredibly successful Hong Kong Sevens.

The pages are crammed with bright pictures of young people displaying the mixed colour of rugby at its most magnificent. Tokkie would have seen it as a moving tribute to his life and he would have been overjoyed.

Shiggy Konno is quoted from the past as saying, "The Hong Kong Sevens have probably done more to elevate rugby, motivate young players and spread the love of the game than any other event."

Tokkie is praised as a founder although he is not included in any of the photographs. He is credited with "suggesting the original notion of seven-a-side teams" and is praised for "completing the huge task of organising the first Hong Kong Sevens in 1976". He is quoted as having said back then "I felt as though I had tried to grab a ball from the middle of a scrum of Lions."

This somewhat described the way he lived his life but in their own interests his fellow elite had effectively reduced him to a footnote in rugby history.

The end of the 1990s were memorable years of action. They brought a final end to apartheid, the British return of Hong Kong to China and notably the beginning of professional rugby.

Curiously, all of these conflicting factors which gave Tokkie such a turbulent life, resolved themselves in 1997. The National Party, which seized power in his youth, finally disbanded in South Africa, confirming the demise of the hated apartheid.

IRB had made that momentous decision in Paris to end the sacred amateur rugby quest and admitting defeat to big money. Professional rugby was introduced that season in Hong Kong, resolving the years of international financial squabbles by which Tokkie had been consumed.

That year also the handover to China ended the last vestiges of the privileged life Tokkie had enjoyed as a member of the colonial rugby establishment and fought so hard to retain.

Any remaining old amateur rugby duffers, no doubt quietly packed their loot from the colonial years, slipped away to other lands and retired to their rose-covered cottages and local pubs.

He never saw Nelson Mandela in public nor the end of apartheid. It would be a decade after Tokkie's death when the freed leader famously donned the green and gold Springbok shirt at the World Cup final in Cape Town, so humanely and generously demonstrating his inclusive nature.

While he was incarcerated on Robben Island for all those years he had watched some fellow prisoners playing improvised rugby with rolled-up rags. He thought it was ironic that rugby was also the revered game of the Afrikaner oppressor community and he had determined to use sport as a way to move towards a multi-racial country.

Tokkie would have been at that great final; no way in the world he would have missed it. His whole life after originally leaving South Africa had been devoted to promoting rugby played together by all people. The Sevens were a beacon of hope in the middle of the apartheid struggle in rugby.

Now on that remarkable World Cup afternoon, back in his beloved South Africa, he would have welcomed the concept of the Rainbow Nation. Surely he deserved to be there and to witness this personally redeeming event? Tokkie would smile, brush away a tear and quietly down another beer.

In August 2016 at Rio de Janiero Games, Fiji won the first Olympic men's gold medal for Sevens Rugby, crushing Great Britain 43-7 in the final. South Africa, long reinstated, received the bronze.

Acknowledgments

FIRST and foremost, I acknowledge Kevin McDonald, who is my advisor, editor and general mentor in the production of this book.

Meeting Kevin in Australia was yet another fortunate rugby story. Long ago, in student days, Willie Jones who played scrum half for London Hospital and Woodford, introduced me to the game and got me into their Extra, Extra B side. He later had a distinguished medical career in Australia and we remained lifelong friends.

Chatting with Kevin and his wife Pat, his relatives at Noosa on Queensland's Sunshine Coast, we were delighted to learn Kevin was not only a rugger enthusiast but a career long professional editor. He immediately offered to help with the book. Thank you, Kevin, for all your support. It is a pleasure working with you.

The Tokkie saga happened way in the past.

While visiting Hong Kong several years ago. I mentioned that Tokkie had been a close friend and proudly that I had played with him a few times for the Colony. Also like him I have a Sevens mug, although admittedly both of us for winning the original Blarney Stone Sevens.

No one seemed to know very much about him except that he had been founder of the Sevens and a sound Football Club member. To make matters worse, the Rugby Union had thoughtlessly lost all its records of those decades.

When we got back to West Vancouver just out of interest I did some research but came up with very little more written about him. This was intriguing and disappointing because he had devoted his whole life to rugby,

The Sevens were well established when l last had dinner with him and Terry in Hong Kong. Then we lost contact until I heard, sometime

Tokkie, the author and book team member Bob D'Eith enjoy a drink together, a while ago.

after the fact, he had died too young in 1985. The obvious answer to my curiosity was to ask contemporaries what had gone on in his later life. As I had known so many of them I expected it to be easy. However, he was already 50 when he died which would now place contemporaries in their 80s. I called around but soon found that depressingly few are still with us. Fortunately I found some very helpful youngsters who were present then and filled gaps in the story.

Several friends have volunteered their Tokkie memories but I particularly acknowledge the contributions of his sister Beth Narain, Chris Wynne-Potts, Ro Hindson, Song Koon Poh, Alamoni Liava'a, Mike Luke, Sandy Muston, Jeremy Wilson and Jim Robinson.

My many talented son Bob D'Eith is always my friend and lawyer but as a successful author himself could offer particular advice. More professional and welcomed family help came from our nephew Oliver Mallich who set up our website and things technical.

Lane, my wife, never met Tokkie but certainly knows him well after years living with him! As always thank you all so much for your affection and support.

The Hong Kong Football Club and Rugby Union management have been very helpful all along and I especially appreciate their permission to reproduce several pictures from their library. Many friends also contributed photographs dug out of their archives and store rooms, several snapped on Brownie cameras.

Some older acquaintances were alarmed my story might depict

Tokkie badly, undoubtedly because they knew him well. Others worried it might show colonial life and the Rugby Union in a bad light. Some just didn't reply. I hope I have not offended but I actually tried to tell the tale from Tokkie's point of view but be balanced about his human failings. Fortunately I have none myself.

I am very aware this is a simplified tale concentrated upon Tokkie while many other unmentioned characters played important roles in the events that happened. I apologise for that, but congratulate them for still being around to protest! Hopefully their memories may correct any mistakes and will add to the Tokkie record.

Much of the material relies upon my diaries which I have kept rather obsessively since my teens and the few boxes of records and photos that have survived Lane's persistent purges.

I relied heavily for general history and continuity upon several popular rugby books and I thank the authors Tony Collins, Kevin Sinclair, John Blondin, Denis Way, Godfrey Robert and Nigel Dunne. Tony particularly helped in encouraging my ideas about the impact of tobacco sponsorship upon rugby.

I was honorary secretary and on the HKRFU committee during the 1960s which provided me with a good background for the story. We did much of the spadework to set up formalised rugby in Asia and develop Hong Kong's contacts around the world. I certainly had my share of tipples with Tokkie and the Old Toffs.

The book turned out to be a fun project. It started out as a dull memorandum of rugby activities and facts. As his story emerged it expanded into colonialism, empire, racism and apartheid. Into booze, infidelity, duplicity, betrayal and tragedy. Throughout, however, it remained focused on his one brilliant achievement: the founding of the Hong Kong Sevens.

While I have obviously taken liberties to lighten up the narrative, everything reported or deduced is based upon my own experiences with Tokkie, a reliable printed source or information from people who knew him. I have put words in his mouth but illustrating actual situations.

I managed to slip in the adventurous rugby icon Erika Roe. I first met my cute little niece Erika in East Africa soon after meeting Tokkie. She was playing on a rug on the lawn of her parents' tea plantation in Njombe, Tanganyika. Yes, niece; my life seems to be one long rugger tale! Thank you Erika for undoubtedly giving Tokkie something to cheer about at a stressful time.

My motivation for writing this book was affection for Tokkie but it is also a salute to the wonderful game of rugby which dominated my life for several years. While I fortunately saw it as a game, Tokkie continued getting more involved and was then totally consumed.

In the so-called golden era of amateur rugby he got no income from his rugby efforts. And for a self-employed businessman this was obviously a formula for disaster. Add an eye for the ladies and a too-quick reach for the bottle and his story develops.

During his whole life, Tokkie was indeed caught up in confusing and changing times. He was a positive man of action, guided by his instincts and desires, which resulted in the dramas but also the wonderful successes of his life.

He would not expect us to take this book too seriously.

I can see him now, chuckling as he reads it, pint in hand.

Cheers, Tokkie!

John D'Eathe,
West Vancouver.
2025

CREATING THE HONG KONG SEVENS

www.ingramcontent.com/pod-product-compliance
Lightning Source LLC
Chambersburg PA
CBHW050328010526
44119CB00050B/716